Your Post-Divorce Compass

Practical, Real-World Advice for the Newly Single

Michael R. Dunham

Contents

✳

Foreword

I wrote this book because it needed to be written.

I have been practicing domestic relations, or "family", law, for more than a decade. The overwhelming majority of these cases end as uncontested cases. The end – as in, the very end, when the divorce decree is signed by the judge and filed with the clerk – is always very anti-climactic to me, and usually to my client, as well. There is no music, no fireworks, no fanfare. Usually it's just my client and me. The only celebration is often me awkwardly congratulating my client.

Soon enough, of course, my client is on her own. My job, which was to have her divorce finalized, is over and done. But I can't help but think her next thought must be, "now what?"

There is an old riddle you have probably heard before – "How do you eat an elephant? … One bite at a time." This book will help you eat the "elephant" of getting on with your life after your divorce. My hope is that working through this book will help you work through your post-divorce life, and that it will leave you feeling better and more capable of approaching the world – and that all that will be done in a month.

The format of this book is fairly simple. In the next few pages, you will see the entire checklist – everything you should be thinking about at some point in making sure your post-divorce life is in order. If you work through the whole list, you will have left no stone unturned. You won't be caught unprepared. You'll never find yourself saying, "gee, I never would have thought of that," about anything coming out of your divorce decree.

Of course, this is not a simple list. While some of the advice I give you can be quickly and easily followed, there are also a number of tasks that are fairly daunting and will take some time. The key, though, is to approach the list systematically and deliberately. We won't take on any more than one task per day. You don't have to do it all at once, and frankly you shouldn't try. If you do, you may find yourself overwhelmed. Part of the purpose of this book is to prevent that from happening.

To that end, every single item on the list has been given a dedicated chapter, with specific instructions and practical advice. Not all of it will apply –

indeed, some tasks can be skipped entirely. But it is easily digestible, enabling you to quickly review it and determine for yourself exactly what you need to do. You can also feel free to skip around; there are only a couple of things I suggest you actually do in a specific order. So if one of the tasks on the list requires you to call a bank, and it's Sunday, skip that one, do something else, and come back to it later. The key is to just keep moving through it.

A note on pronouns – to be completely honest, I have been inspired to write this book by my female clients, and they're who I keep thinking about as I'm writing. That is not a comment on anything other than my own experience. It is certainly not a suggestion that women need more help with this stuff than men, or that men don't need this kind of help. Indeed, if anything, my experience is probably an indictment of the fact that men tend to be less likely to ask for help even when they clearly need it. But my point is that where I refer to "you" in the third person, I will generally (but not necessarily always) use the female pronoun rather than an awkward "his/her" construct or something like that. I think it makes the book more readable, but I don't want anyone thinking this list doesn't apply to men, too.

I hope you find this useful. If you have any questions or would like to provide whatever (constructive) commentary or criticism strikes your fancy, I would love to hear from you – please reach out to me at *info@postdivorcecompass.com* any time. Thanks!

Acknowledgements

In many ways, this book is the product of a community effort, as I have asked a number of people with expertise in various areas to review certain sections and provide me with good, constructive feedback. In no particular order, I would like to thank Karen Vining, Beau Varnadoe, Al Schiebel, Erin Digby, Shelley Elder, Bill Heath, Beth Pitt, and David McDonough for their efforts. I also want to thank my Facebook "hive mind" (too many friends to name) for letting me vet title and other ideas through them.

I'd also like to specially thank Lynn Abent for her valuable help and insight, as well as my mother, Patty Dunham, and Amy Head, who have always been two of my biggest cheerleaders, for reviewing the whole book and giving me more feedback than I ever expected.

And of course, I would like to thank my wife, Donna, and my children, Abby and Jake, for putting up with me when the creative process intrudes on real life.

How to Use This Book

To understand what this book *is*, it is important to understand what this book is *not*:

➤ This book is not about coping with your divorce emotionally. There are lots of resources for that, including:

- *Books*. There are literally thousands of available titles that can help you. Brittany Wong of The Huffington Post has a good list here: *http://www.huffingtonpost.com/2015/06/05/books-to-read-during-divorce_n_7522458.html*

- *Trained Professionals*. The assistance of a counselor, life coach, psychologist, and/or psychiatrist can be invaluable. There is no shame in at least talking with someone, and I am a strong believer that pretty much everyone who goes through a divorce should speak with a counselor at some point.

- *Religious Figures*. If you are looking for "faith-based" assistance, you might speak with your priest, minister, pastor, rabbi, or other religious leader.

- *Support Groups*. There may be one in your area that can provide assistance in a group setting.

If you need help dealing with your emotional or spiritual health, that is more important than anything you will read in *this* book. Get whatever help you need, from anywhere you can get it.

➤ This book is not about co-parenting or dealing with issues relating to your children and/or your former spouse. There are several good books about that subject, also, as well as parenting and co-parenting classes that you can take.

➤ This book is not about dating or your other relationships after your divorce. The only advice I can give you on that subject is to force yourself to slow down, especially if you have children.

➤ This book is not about helping you figure out "what went wrong" – or worse, "what you did wrong" – during your marriage. Those questions may be worth asking before you become involved in another long-term, committed relationship, but there are other resources for helping you work through those issues.

What this book *does* contain is information which is much more pragmatic and will help you sort out the nuts and bolts of your everyday life. We will address things like making sure your insurance needs are met, straightening out your banking, and remembering to update your driver's license. We will look at some areas you might not have thought about, like updating online passwords, shredding old documents, and fixing the title to your house. And we will try to think beyond the immediate as we explore repairing your credit score and your financial life, as well as building a team of advisors who will serve your financial needs for years to come.

Another theme of this book is that I don't want you to feel like the list of things to do is more than you can handle. By spreading out the tasks on the list over a series of days, you will be able to get everything done. It's all about being intentional and consistent, and if you work systematically, you will get everything done, in surprisingly little time.

With that being said, I want to stress that many of the tasks I describe here cannot be completed in a single day. A great example of this is Day 13, "Get Your QDROs Done". The task list for Day 13 includes doing some research with a retirement plan administrator, drafting a court order, getting a judge to sign and file that order, and then getting the order in the hands of the plan administrator. It should be obvious that can't possibly be done in a day. What "Day 13" means is two-fold:

1.   You should **START** the task described in this chapter on Day 13.

2.   You should **WAIT UNTIL** Day 13 to start the task described in this chapter.

In some cases, it's entirely possible you could do two or three chapters or even more in a single day. But the focus of this book is on being intentional and deliberate, so that you don't become overwhelmed.

Before you continue, get a calendar. Even if you already have one, I want you to get another one. It should be paper-based, even if your world is digital. There are templates available in Appendix A of this book and at *www.postdivorcecompass.com*. Start it with today's date and fill it out three months in advance. You're going to use it to keep track of everything you're doing as you work through this book. If you want to plan to destroy it when you're done, that's okay – you can even make a little mini-ceremony out of it.

When you start a chapter, write "Begin Day (X)!" on the appropriate day on your calendar. The challenge will be to try and keep a continuous chain of "Begin" notations on your calendar. In this way, you'll be able to see your progress, which will motivate you to keep going.

When you finish that chapter, write "Day (X) done!" on the appropriate day on your calendar. This will motivate you, too, as you continue to cross things off your list.

Before Your Divorce is Finalized

In all likelihood, by the time you got your hands on a copy of this book, your divorce was already finalized. Hopefully, everything on the short list that follows, you already did. If not, however, try to go back and do these things if you can, even if it means you need to reopen your divorce (which is usually difficult to do anyway).

1. **If you want your maiden name back, make sure you have that done in the divorce decree.** You can probably have this done as a matter of right as part of your divorce, and it will cost you nothing extra to do it this way. However, once your divorce is finalized, changing your name will probably require a new legal proceeding, which will cost you money and take a few months to accomplish. It's much easier to have this taken care of in the divorce decree, so don't forget to have this done.

2. **You should have opened a new checking account, in your own name.** If you already had one in your own name, which your spouse never had his name on or access to, great. But if you had joint accounts all along, you should open your own checking account as soon as possible, if you haven't already done so. I strongly recommend you use a bank that neither you nor your spouse ever had a relationship with; that way some confused teller won't give your spouse access to your account information because there are other joint accounts "in their system".

3. **Decide how you're going to celebrate when you're done, and put it on the calendar and/or buy what you need to make that happen.** Maybe it's a bottle of wine. Maybe it's a movie. It doesn't have to be huge or expensive; all you're doing is setting a goal. When you decide, write it down here:

I'm going to celebrate the end of my post-divorce journey by:

_____

_____

The List

Okay, let's get to it: here's the whole list. Again, please keep one thing in mind – I don't recommend trying to plow through the whole thing in one sitting, or over just a few hours or days. Maybe you can handle doing things that way, but the odds are that you can't. I would rather you take your time, be methodical, and patiently work through it. You'll still be done in just a couple of months, which is pretty quick in the grand scheme of things.

Day 1: Automate Support Payments

Day 2: Get an Income Deduction Order

Day 3: Pull Your Credit Reports

Day 4: Verify Joint Accounts Have Been Closed

Day 5: Notify Creditors of Name Change and/or Change of Address

Day 6: Update Your Social Security Card

Day 7: Update Your Driver's License and/or Passport

Day 8: Change Online Passwords

Day 9: Open a Savings Account

Day 10: Get a Credit Card and Set Up a Recurring Payment

Day 11: Change Beneficiaries on Retirement Accounts

Day 12: Change Beneficiaries on Life Insurance Policies

Day 13: Get Your QDROs Done

Day 14: Get Health Insurance

Day 15: Get Life Insurance

Day 16: Get Umbrella Insurance

Day 17: Update Your Estate Plan

Day 18: Refinance Your Mortgage or Sign a New Lease

Day 19: Retitle Your House

Day 20: Retitle Your Car

Day 21: Update ALL Your Insurance

Day 22: Get a Tax Accountant

Day 23: Get a Financial Planner

Day 24: Buy a Cross-Cut Shredder and Put It to Work

Day 25: Get a Safe Deposit Box or Personal Fireproof Safe

Day 26: Get Extra Certified Copies of Important Documents

Day 27: Get Proof of Life Insurance from Your Spouse

Day 28: Go Through Every Room in Your Home

Day 29: Put Together a Basic Debt Payoff Plan

Day 30: Review Your Divorce Paperwork, One More Time

I know it's a lot to take in. That's why I've systematized it the way I have in this book. Believe me, you can do this.

We'll get started in a minute, but first I want you to take 60 seconds and write down how you're feeling about this process. Set a timer if you have to. Don't think, just write. Ready? GO!

_____

_____

_____

_____

_____

_____

Now, let's get started.

✳

Day 1: Automate Support Payments

If you're obligated to pay child support or alimony, making those payments is the most important thing in your life until that obligation goes away. You're ordered by the Court to make those payments, so if you miss one, bad things are almost sure to follow. You could find your wages subject to garnishment. There could be interest (at staggering rates, comparable to a bad credit card) or other financial penalties. In some states, you could lose your driver's license. You can also be sanctioned by the Court in whatever way the Court sees fit – which can include jail time.

Here's the best way to avoid those bad things happening:

1. **Open a joint account with a minimum deposit, ideally at your former spouse's bank.** This is where the payments will be deposited. That way, you'll be able to go to the records for that account and easily get a complete list of all your payments. Note that you will never, ever be able to spend any of the money you put in this account, so if the bank sends you checks or debit cards for this account, either destroy them or give them to your former spouse.

   DONE on _____!

2. **Find out if your employer can directly deposit funds from your paycheck to this new joint account.** Employers are often set up for this kind of thing, which is essentially the same thing as a wage garnishment or an income deduction order. Don't assume an employer who happens to be a small business can't handle this kind of thing; to the contrary, such businesses often use payroll servicing companies that can handle this sort of thing as a matter of routine. There will be some paperwork for you to fill out, and there may be a nominal administrative charge (which you should only have to pay one time, not on a recurring basis).

   Some people are reluctant to involve their employers in these kinds of things. In most cases, I would suggest you get over it. There is virtually no chance your employer is unaware of your divorce, and an even lesser chance (usually) that they actually care. Unless you work for a business that believes its employees' marital status somehow reflects on that business's image, your employer is probably far more interested in you helping them make money than in your personal life.

Once this kind of thing is set up one time, the employer doesn't have any "extra" work to do from paycheck to paycheck to process this kind of thing. Some employers may even be impressed that you're proactively automating something like this so you will be less likely to be distracted in the future.

DONE on _____!

3.   **Write a letter or an email to your former spouse explaining what you've set up.** Ideally you have already had this conversation with her anyway. If you've set this account up at her bank, transferring the payments from this joint account to her personal account should be easy. Just be sure she is aware that she should not let the balance in this account fall below the minimum necessary to keep the account open (which should be whatever amount you were initially required to deposit to open the account).

DONE on _____!

If you are the recipient of child support and/or alimony, you should consider working with your former spouse to make sure he does all of these things. You can go ahead and open the joint account at your bank, which is separate from your personal account. You should provide him with the account information in writing as quickly as possible, and you should direct him to deposit his support payments directly into this account.

You should not, however, use this account for anything else. Once the money is deposited into this account, you should transfer it over to your own account and spend it from there. If it ever becomes necessary to litigate over support payments, you'll appreciate the fact you kept the transaction history on this particular account "clean" by limiting it to the transfer of support payments and nothing else.

NEXT PAGE

Check one:

_____   **I finished this step on _____(date)_____ and marked "Day 1" on my calendar.**

_____   **This step did not apply to me because _____**

_____

_____.

STOP – Day 1 is complete. Good work!

Day 2: Get an Income Deduction Order

Many states provide for support payments to be automatically deducted from the payor's wages, through the use of a specialized court order typically known as an "income deduction order" or "income withholding order" (which I will call an "IDO" for now). An IDO functions the same as a wage garnishment, with one major additional advantage – unlike a garnishment action which may need to be renewed every six months or so, an IDO will remain in place for much longer and does not have to be renewed. This is the other side of the coin we explored in Day 1, and the reason to do it is the same – if you can automate these payments, then you will have predictable personal cash flow, which can not only save time but also bring peace of mind.

Here's how to do it:

1. **Determine whether you are eligible to have an IDO entered in the first place.** The first question is whether an IDO is available to you. Your state probably has a default rule one way or the other, so you should know that rule. You will also need to review your divorce agreement and/or divorce decree, to be sure your state's default rule has not been overridden. In a state where the default rule is for an IDO to be entered, it is common for the payor to negotiate a waiver of that requirement into his divorce agreement. If that has been done, then you can't get an IDO right away, but there will likely be conditions written in under which you can get one, so you'll need to watch for those conditions.

   Here's an example of what I'm talking about, from standard language I include in my own agreements:

   > *"The Parties agree it is not in the best interests of the Children for an income deduction order to be entered at this time. However, should child support payments directly to a Party required hereunder not be timely paid, or if there has been a failure to make support payments due so that the amount unpaid is equal to or greater than the amount payable for one month, the Court may enter an income deduction order at the request of the Party to whom support payments are owed."*

In other words, if the payee does not receive the payments on time, or if a month goes by with no payment at all, then she can apply directly to the Court for an IDO.

DONE on _____!

2. **Assuming you are eligible, draft the IDO.** You should consider having an attorney help you with this step, but this is something you can do yourself, if you want. Don't reinvent this wheel – do an internet search for something like "sample form income deduction order [STATE]" and you should find plenty of sample documents. Make sure you include all of the following:

➤ The style of your case, or some other reference to your specific case including jurisdiction and case number

➤ Your former spouse's name and address as "payor" (but do NOT include his Social Security number or birth date; you can and should provide this information separately, not in this order, which will become public record)

➤ Your name as "payee"

➤ If the IDO includes child support payments, your children's names and dates of birth (years only to help protect their identities)

➤ A statement as to when the IDO becomes effective (usually "immediately")

➤ A statement as to when the IDO expires (could be when your children turn 18 and/or graduate from high school, or when your alimony is set to expire, or some other date certain)

➤ The amount to be withheld per month or other period, which should include any applicable processing fees

➤ Designation of payment of processing fees, if applicable

➤ Directions on where and how payments should be sent

➤ A statement regarding the applicability of the federal Consumer Protection Act

➤ Other statements and directions that may be required in your specific state

Again, this is a relatively simple document, but it is also somewhat technical, so consider having an attorney help you prepare it.

DONE on _____!

3. **Prepare any other documents required by your state for an IDO to be entered and processed correctly.** If a governmental entity is involved in the collection of the payments (which may be required by law, depending on your state), there is almost certainly other paperwork that will have to be filled out.

    DONE on _____!

4. **Forward the IDO to the Court, with a cover letter asking for a certified copy to be mailed back to you.** Include a self-addressed stamped envelope so the Court can mail your copy back to you.

    DONE on _____!

5. **Once you have a certified copy of your IDO in hand, send it to your former spouse's employer's payroll or human resources department.** For a small company, this could be the president or owner of the company. Make sure you include a cover letter with instructions consistent with the IDO; this is where you will include your former spouse's Social Security number and birth date, as well. Be sure to send a copy of all of these documents to your former spouse.

    DONE on _____!

6. **Once you can confirm the IDO is in place and the employer is withholding money and paying it over to you, follow up with your former spouse if there is an outstanding support balance that may have accrued in the interim.** Sometimes, the former spouse will neglect to pay support once he finds out an IDO has been entered, but it will take a few weeks for the employer to actually process it. Hopefully this will be the product of an honest mistake about the timing of the automatic deduction, but even if it's

not, you will need to have made this request in writing before you can do anything more serious to try and collect it.

DONE on _____!

An attorney will handle all of this for you, if you want. For a decent attorney, all of the above is a matter of routine. You can do this yourself if you want or need to save a little money, but if you can afford it, you may want to have an attorney do it just to be sure it is done correctly.

That said, if you want to try and handle it yourself, there are sample forms and letters in Appendix B that you might want to check out.

Check one:

_____   **I finished this step on _____(date)_____ and marked "Day 2" on my calendar.**

_____   **This step did not apply to me because _____**

_____

_____.

STOP – Day 2 is complete. Good work!

Day 3: Pull Your Credit Reports

Your credit report contains a ton of information about you – frankly, it's scary just how much is there. This report contains virtually every piece of information creditors and others use to make financial decisions about you, not only relating to the extension of credit, but even for such things as employment, whether to lease an apartment to you, or whether and how to rate you for insurance purposes. Given how big a role these reports play in your life, it is surprising how many people never bother to look at them.

Though it is recommended that you review your credit report every year, even if you don't do that, immediately after a major life event – such as your divorce – is a great time to do so. There are three main credit reporting agencies (Equifax, Experian, and TransUnion), and by federal law they each have to provide you with one free copy of the reports they generate on you once per year.

The good news is, getting your free copy of each report is ridiculously easy. The three companies jointly operate the web site, *www.AnnualCreditReport.com*, which allows you to obtain all three reports online. All you have to do is go to that site, click the "Request your free credit reports" button on the home page, and follow the directions on the site. You can get them online, or they have a form for you to fill out and mail in, if you would prefer to receive your reports by mail.

NOTE: This site is the only site that is (a) truly free, (b) free forever (as long as you limit yourself to one report per year), and (c) operated by the actual reporting agencies themselves. There are many, many other sites promising credit reporting to you, but typically you have to provide them with a credit card so that they can start charging you for other services (e.g., identity theft protection, or alerts whenever someone pulls your score), which you may or may not want. Whether these services are appropriate for you is out of scope for this book, so you will have to do your own research. But for purposes of what I'm asking you do here, all you need is your credit reports, one time.

So now that you have your credit reports, here's what you do next:

1.   **Read them.** Even if you like doing everything paperless, I'd recommend getting a highlighter or a pen and a pad of post-it notes and start going through them, line by line. When you find something

you don't understand or that doesn't seem right, highlight it and flag it so you can come back to it. Do NOT stop and do any research on it right now; just highlight issues you don't understand. Do this for all three reports.

DONE on _____!

2.   **Get a pad of paper and go back through the reports, writing out all of the issues you found in one place.** As you go through the second and third reports, if you find the same issue in one report that you found in another, you can just note that the same issue appears in both reports, rather than treating them as two separate issues.

DONE on _____!

3.   **Start working the phones.** You will want to take good notes regarding who you talked with and when, and what you discussed, and what they say they will do for you or send to you. Make sure you get good information on where to send written correspondence on these matters (ideally including an email address). If they give you a P.O. Box, make sure you get a physical address also, in case you need to send them something using a delivery service (e.g., FedEx) later, as those services will typically not deliver to a P.O. Box.

DONE on _____!

4.   **Use your notes to write letters or emails confirming your conversations.** You always want to follow up your telephone conversations with creditors in writing. The goal is to have these items eventually removed from your credit reports, and if the creditor is slow to act (or totally uncooperative), you will want your own file so you can go directly to the credit reporting agency.

DONE on _____!

5.   **For debts that are your former spouse's responsibility, write him a letter or email asking him to resolve them.** Ideally, these specific debts are listed in your divorce agreement or divorce decree. If that's the case, then if your former spouse does not act to resolve them, he can be sanctioned by the Court later.

DONE on _____!

6. **Work with the creditor (as necessary) to come up with a plan to retire any debts that are legitimately your responsibility.** Sometimes, this is as simple as continuing to pay off your mortgage every month. Other times, you may be trying to resolve a debt that has lingered for a long time and is dragging down your credit score. Creditors are often more understanding than you may expect, particularly if you are making a good faith effort. Be creative in proposing solutions; creditors have been known to reduce or write off some of the debt (especially ancillary charges like interest, late fees, or collection fees) if you commit to regular payments and/or can pay a lump sum. Follow these three guiding principles:

    ➤ Don't commit to something that isn't realistic for you.

    ➤ Whatever you work out with any creditor should be reduced to writing. If you work it out over the phone, that's okay – just follow it up with a letter or an email, and be able to prove it was delivered to the creditor.

    ➤ Once you do reach an agreement with a creditor, do whatever you can to automate those payments so that you don't have to worry about it any more.

    DONE on _____!

7. **Calendar yourself to pull your credit reports again next year so you can check your progress.** For this exercise, you pulled all three at once. Since you can only do this for free once a year, you might want to space them out for next year. For instance, if you are doing this in January this year, next year you might want to pull one of them in January, one from a different agency in May, and one from the third agency in September, so that you can check on one every four months instead of checking them all once every twelve months.

NEXT PAGE

Check one:

_____ I finished this step on _____(date)_____ and marked "Day 3" on my calendar.

_____ This step did not apply to me because _____

_____

_____.

STOP – Day 3 is complete. Good work!

Day 4: Verify Joint Accounts Have Been Closed

Hopefully this one is easy, as it should have been done by the time your divorce was finalized. Still, it's worth making sure, just in case.

1. **Get a copy of your divorce decree and/or agreement to bring with you.** Hopefully it addresses what, specifically, is supposed to happen with each and every joint account you ever had.

   DONE on _____!

2. **Go visit a branch of the bank (credit union, etc.) where the account was held.** You probably won't be able to get far over the phone. Ideally you will have the account number(s), your divorce decree and/or agreement, and your driver's license or other ID.

   DONE on _____!

3. **If there are funds in the account that belong to you, withdraw them.** Of course, you should first confirm that there are no outstanding checks that have not yet cleared the account, unless the checks are "stale". Ask your bank what it considers a "stale" check. Usually it's 3-6 months but it can be as long as one year or more.

   You can either take cash or get the bank to issue you a cashier's check or a bank check. If it's a large sum, you're better off getting a check, for your security. Note that the bank may want to charge you a fee for a cashier's check or a bank check, but if you ask them to waive that fee, they usually will, especially if you tell them you'll take cash instead if they insist on the fee.

   DONE on _____!

4. **If there are funds in the account that belong to your former spouse, ask him to withdraw them.** You should also notify the bank that you do not wish to be held responsible for any liability associated with this account. You may need to show the bank a copy of your divorce decree and ask them to flag the account.

   If your former spouse is uncooperative, you have a couple of options.

   ➤ Least advisable would be to take the funds for yourself. If your former spouse later asks for the funds, you can probably be compelled to pay them over to him if the divorce paperwork clearly awards them to him.

➤ It may be practical to have the bank issue a cashier's check or bank check payable to him and then deliver that check to him – ensuring, of course, that you use some means that enables you to prove delivery (e.g., FedEx or some other courier or delivery service). If you know where your former spouse lives or works, this is probably your best option.

➤ You could ask the bank for their input and assistance. The bank may have policies and procedures for what happens under these circumstances. For example, the bank may impose a "freeze" on the account, which would require a bank officer to approve future transactions involving that account. While that would not necessarily result in the account being closed, it will ensure transactions on that account that may create liability for you can't happen in the future.

Your divorce decree and/or agreement likely contains language directing both spouses to cooperate with each other to effectuate the terms of the divorce documents. If your former spouse continues to refuse to cooperate, you can consider seeking contempt sanctions to compel him to obey the Court's orders.

DONE on _____!

5. **Direct the bank to close the account.** Make sure the bank gives you written documentation confirming the account has in fact been closed.

DONE on _____!

6. **Ask the bank to verify there are no other joint accounts which remain open.** If there are, repeat steps 3-5 for each of those accounts, as well.

DONE on _____!

7. **Repeat Steps 2-6 with other banks.** To be on the safe side, you should repeat this process with every bank where you and your spouse ever had a joint account. You should also review your credit report

and check with all of the banks and other financial institutions you find there, too.

DONE on _____!

8. **Don't forget about credit cards and other unsecured debts.**
If you and your former spouse had joint credit cards, you should go ahead and close them. However, if the card was originally yours and your former spouse was merely an "authorized user", then consider canceling only his authorization to use your card, and any separate card which may have been issued to him, rather than closing the entire account.

The reason for this is that you want to keep open your own accounts, especially if they have been open for some time, to avoid hurting your credit score. A major factor in calculating your credit score is the length of your credit history, and if you close the cards that have been open the longest, your credit score will drop immediately, even though you have arguably made yourself *less* risky by minimizing your total liability. You are better off keeping the card open and using it intermittently, even if you don't plan on maintaining credit card debt (which is smart).

On the other hand, if you know you were merely an "authorized user" on a card belonging to your former spouse, then all you should do is cancel your own card and notify the creditor in writing that you are no longer responsible for the account. Provide a copy of your divorce decree and/or agreement if necessary.

Obviously, if there is debt against the card, that will have to be resolved. Your divorce decree and/or agreement should specify who is responsible for payment of the debt. However, even if there is debt, you should be able to close – or at least freeze – the account, to ensure the debt cannot be increased.

NEXT PAGE

Check one:

_____   **I finished this step on _____(date)_____ and marked "Day 4" on my calendar.**

_____   **This step did not apply to me because _____**

_____

_____.

STOP – Day 4 is complete. Good work!

Day 5: Notify Creditors of Name Change and/or Change of Address

If your name changed, or if you moved, or both, then you will need to notify your creditors. You should draw up a simple "form letter" and then send letters to all of the following:

- ➤ Every creditor listed on your credit report
- ➤ Every creditor you currently have, even if they're not listed on your credit report
- ➤ Every bank or other financial institution where you have an account
- ➤ All of your utilities servicing your home

In most cases, it will be sufficient for you to send these notice letters by regular mail. Keep a list so you know when and to whom you mailed notice letters, and allow several weeks for them to process the change. If, after a couple of months, you notice a change has not been made, you should call that creditor to find out if you sent the notice letter to the correct address.

If you need the notice letter to arrive quickly or by a certain date, or if you are sending a notice letter to a creditor for the second time, or if for whatever reason it is extra important to you to be able to confirm that a notice letter was delivered, then you should go ahead and use a courier service such as FedEx. Note that if you do so, you will not be able to deliver to a P.O. Box or other "mail drop", but rather you will have to have a physical address. Generally it is fairly easy to find this information from the creditor's web site, or you can call the creditor to get it.

NEXT PAGE

Check one:

_____ **I finished this step on _____(date)_____ and marked "Day 5" on my calendar.**

_____ **This step did not apply to me because _____**

_____

_____.

STOP – Day 5 is complete. Good work!

Day 6: Update Your Social Security Card

If you reverted to your maiden name, you will need to update your Social Security card. This is a fairly straightforward process. Here's what you have to do:

1. **Make sure you did, in fact, get your maiden name back.** If it's not in your divorce decree, then you'll need to see if you can get that corrected, which is probably only possible if you were divorced *very* recently. If you can't get it corrected in your divorce decree, then you will probably need to file a separate name change petition in the jurisdiction where you live and get a final decree of name change first.

    DONE on _____!

2. **Get a certified copy of your divorce decree.** A regular copy won't work; it has to be a "certified" copy from the Clerk of the Court. You should expect that you won't get this one back once you send it to the Social Security office.

    DONE on _____!

3. **Download a copy of the "Application for a Social Security Card", print it out, and fill it out.** The link, as of this writing, is:

    www.socialsecurity.gov/forms/ss-5.pdf

    DONE on _____!

4. **Mail the completed Application and the certified copy of your divorce decree to the Social Security office as directed.** Alternatively, if you wish, you can take it to your local Social Security office, if that's convenient for you.

    DONE on _____!

Your new card will probably arrive in a couple of weeks. Pay special attention to checking the mail until it arrives, to minimize the chance that it is stolen by an identity thief.

NEXT PAGE

Check one:

_____   **I finished this step on _____(date)_____ and marked "Day 6" on my calendar.**

_____   **This step did not apply to me because _____**

_____

_____.

STOP – Day 6 is complete. Good work!

Day 7: Update Your Driver's License and/or Passport

If your name or address changed, you'll need to update your driver's license (and your passport, if you have a passport). This process is very similar to what you may have done on Day 6.

To change your driver's license, the first thing you should do is an internet search for something like "update driver's license divorce [STATE]" for specific instructions in your state. In general, however, the process will probably look something like this:

1. **You'll need a certified copy of your divorce decree.** A change in your driver's license which is based on a divorce might be free of charge, which is why you'll need your divorce decree. A "regular" copy is not good enough. Note that if your name changed, your divorce decree will have to show the restoration of your maiden name.

2. **If your address changed, you'll need proof of your new residence address.** This can vary depending on your state, but usually a copy of your lease or new deed and a copy of a utility bill servicing the new address will suffice.

3. **Bring these documents to the nearest DMV office.** In most states, you have to do this in person and can't do it over the phone, online, or via the mail.

To change your passport, you will have to have it reissued. You will need your current passport, a certified copy of your divorce decree, and a color passport photo. You'll also need to fill out some paperwork. Detailed instructions and the forms you'll need are available from the State Department's web site here:

travel.state.gov/content/passports/english/passports/services/correction.html

NEXT PAGE

Check one:

_____ **I finished this step on _____(date)_____ and marked "Day 7" on my calendar.**

_____ **This step did not apply to me because _____**

_____

_____.

STOP – Day 7 is complete. Good work!

Day 8: Change Online Passwords

If you haven't done so already, you should change your passwords for everything you use online, especially if there is even the remotest chance your former spouse ever knew any of them.

Ideally your passwords are unique for every web site (meaning, you don't use the same password for two different sites – let alone all of them), have no obvious personal connection to you (e.g., your dog's name), and are difficult to guess. An increasing number of web sites are requiring you to use combinations of lowercase letters, uppercase letters, numbers, *and* punctuation marks, and to be of a certain length (usually at least 8-10 characters long). In many cases (e.g., for your bank, credit card, or car loan) it makes sense to do this even if the site doesn't force you to create such a strong password. The downside to doing this, of course, is that it can be difficult to remember all of these passwords.

Here's a strategy that will give you reasonably strong passwords that you should be able to remember without too much difficulty:

1. **Come up with your own personal, difficult-to-guess passphrase.** I would suggest using two or three short words that create a mental picture in your mind that is easy to remember, most likely because it is ridiculous. For example, you could pick "`giant purple monkey`".

2. **Modify the passphrase by capitalizing the first letter of each word and removing the spaces.** So now our passphrase is "`GiantPurpleMonkey`".

3. **Add the three-letter prefix of your phone number.** Let's say your phone number is 212-555-1234 – the "prefix" is "555". Now our passphrase is "`GiantPurpleMonkey555`".

4. **Add a "special character", such as a period or an underscore.** Now you have (for instance) "`GiantPurpleMonkey555$`".

5. **For each web site, take the first five letters of the domain name.** For *www.amazon.com*, the "domain name" is *amazon.com*, so the first five letters would be "amazo". If the domain name has less than

five letters – e.g., Barnes and Noble's site is *www.bn.com* - just take the whole domain name ("bn", in this case).

6. **Add this little bit of the domain name to your passphrase, and you have an easily remembered, yet unique password for that web site.** Using these two sites as examples, our passwords would be "`GiantPurpleMonkey555$amazo`" and "`GiantPurpleMonkey555$bn`". These are strong passwords that would be nearly impossible to guess and would satisfy all but the most rigorous of password requirements – and yet remembering them is fairly easy.

You can, of course, use a rule of reason for some of this. You may have several sites where you need a password but really aren't all that concerned about keeping it secure – for example, a password on your "account" that you need to leave a comment on a blog site or to read an article. For these, it is perfectly fine for you to pick an easily memorable password and just use the same one for everything. Just be logical and reasonable about it (and at the very least, don't use "password" or any variant of that word).

Check one:

_____   **I finished this step on _____(date)_____ and marked "Day 8" on my calendar.**

_____   **This step did not apply to me because _____**

_____

_____.

STOP – Day 8 is complete. Good work!

36

Day 9: Open a Savings Account

You almost certainly opened your own checking account before your divorce was finalized. If you didn't, I recommended you open one before starting to work on this list. If you got this far and *still* haven't opened your own checking account, you should go do that now.

Assuming you have a checking account, your activity for today is to open a savings account linked to your checking account. You will probably need a minimum deposit of something like $10 or $25. It should be as easy as filling out a form and asking your banker to set it up for you, which should be easily accomplished in a thirty-minute trip to the bank. Make sure you ask the bank to link the two accounts together so that the savings account can be used as overdraft protection for the checking account.

In this day and age, a savings account is a terrible investment vehicle that pays either no interest or interest substantially below the inflation rate. Your real goal is to build up an emergency cushion. I would suggest building up savings of $1,000.00 in this account.

If you have enough money, go ahead and deposit that much into this account, and then forget it's there (and skip to the end of this chapter). If you don't, deposit what you can and try and figure out how you can build this up over time. There are lots of strategies for doing this. Just a few examples:

➤ Commit to transferring some regular amount – $100, $50, even $10 or $20 if that's all you can afford – every month, or every time you get a paycheck. Some banks let you set this up automatically from your direct deposits (e.g., PNC Bank's "Virtual Wallet" product allows you to do this).

➤ Some banks allow you to make automatic transfers to savings whenever you make a transaction in your checking account. For example, Bank of America's "Keep the Change" program rounds every transaction up to the next whole dollar and transfers the difference to your savings (e.g., you spend $4.07 on a latte - $0.93 is transferred to savings).

➤ You could have a yard sale or sell some items on eBay to declutter, and put the proceeds into savings.

➤ You could take on odd jobs or freelance work.

Again, this isn't about building your retirement or anything like that – it's about protecting your finances when something unexpected happens. Maybe you have an unexpected car repair. Maybe you forget a deposit and accidentally bounce a check. If you have this cushion of savings, these kinds of things won't be the emergencies they might be if you didn't have it.

Check one:

_____   **I finished this step on _____(date)_____ and marked "Day 9" on my calendar.**

_____   **This step did not apply to me because _____**

_____

_____.

STOP – Day 9 is complete. Good work!

Day 10: Get a Credit Card and Set Up a Recurring Payment

Going through a divorce will often wreck your credit. Or, depending on your situation, you may not have had much of your own credit history in the first place. Either way, you need to start doing what you can to build or improve your credit history. Like it or not, intelligent use of a credit card is one of the best things you can do.

You can get a credit card practically anywhere, but I usually counsel people to keep things as simple as possible. By now you have a banking relationship with an institution where you have two accounts set up. That's a great place to get a credit card. Again, this is a fairly simple process that probably involves little more than filling out a simple application.

If you're turned down, talk to your banker about what you can do. Explain that you're trying to build or repair your credit history and you're not looking for something complicated or exotic. Your banker should be able to help you find something that will work for you. If all else fails, you should be able to get a secured credit card (i.e., backed by collateral of some sort) – you can use the savings account you set up on Day 9 to secure it. Over time, you should be able to remove the requirement that you have security.

The interest rate will probably be terrible, and the limit may be fairly low. That's okay; neither of those things will impede what we're doing here. Once the card has been issued, here's what I recommend you do with it:

1. **Pick one of your monthly utility payments, ideally one with a fairly regular payment, which is less than the limit on your card and which can be paid by credit card.** Water and sewer, pest control, and trash pickup are good examples in many cases. Electricity and natural gas aren't as good because they can vary highly with the seasons, unless you've enrolled in some sort of "flat billing" program (which some utility companies do offer).

    DONE on _____!

2. **With a copy of your most recent utility bill in hand, go online and set up recurring monthly payments on that card.** Until your credit history has been repaired to some degree, this should

be the only transaction on this card (which is why I told you not to worry about the limit on the card).

DONE on _____!

3. **Make sure you pay off the card every month.** By paying the card off in full every month, you incur no interest charges (which is why I told you not to worry about the terrible interest rate on the card). If you can set it up so the card is paid off automatically, so much the better, as you will not have to spend one second administering this credit repair effort in the future.

DONE on _____!

4. **Put the card somewhere safe.** You can use a dresser drawer, wall safe, freezer, or whatever makes sense to you. The point is to pick someplace where the card is safe and secure, and more importantly, out of your sight (which will put it out of your mind).

DONE on _____!

If you have the discipline to control your spending and pay off the balances every month, credit cards can be powerful financial allies. However, assuming you're still trying to rebuild your life and don't have much experience running your own finances, following this process will build your credit history in a safe, controlled manner and will keep you out of trouble.

Check one:

_____   **I finished this step on _____(date)_____ and marked "Day 10" on my calendar.**

_____   **This step did not apply to me because _____**

_____

_____.

STOP – Day 10 is complete. Good work!

PAUSE AND REFLECT

You've been at it for about a week and a half, and you're a third of the way done. Take a moment and reflect on what you've been able to accomplish in so little time:

➤ You have automated your support payments so that you don't have to think about them any more.

➤ You have pulled your credit reports and reviewed them to make sure anything on any of them that is not your responsibility has been addressed.

➤ You've verified all of your joint accounts have been closed.

➤ You've notified all of your creditors and the Social Security office that your name and/or address have changed.

➤ You updated your driver's license and your passport.

➤ You updated all of your online passwords so your former spouse can't access your accounts.

➤ You opened a savings account and started building your personal emergency fund.

➤ You started repairing your credit by opening a brand-new credit card and automated a payment that will help build your credit history over time.

That's a lot of stuff, and you should be proud! Before you keep going, though, you should take a moment and reflect. How do you feel? Take 60 seconds and write down how you're feeling about this process so far. Set a timer if you have to. Again, don't think, just write. Ready? GO!

_____

_____

_____

NOW you can keep going. Good work!

✳

Day 11: Change Beneficiaries on Retirement Accounts

Your divorce decree and/or agreement should have expressly stated that your retirement accounts were awarded to you, and that your former spouse would have no interest in them. That's a good start, but you still need to notify the account holders.

1.   **Make a list of all your accounts.** In addition to typical retirement accounts like IRA's and 401(k) accounts, don't forget about other financial vehicles like annuities, pensions, and stock accounts.

     DONE on _____!

2.   **Contact the plan administrator for each account and ask them to send you whatever paperwork you need to change the beneficiary in the event of a divorce.** Hopefully they can email it to you or direct you to an online resource. In some cases, all they need is a simple letter requesting the change. Be sure to get exact instructions on where to send the completed paperwork.

     DONE on _____!

3.   **Get certified copies of your divorce decree, enough to send one to each institution that requires it.** For some types of accounts, you may not need to prove to the institution that you are divorced (e.g., an IRA typically does not have this requirement).

     DONE on _____!

4.   **Fill out the paperwork and send it in.** You might be able to do this online, but most likely not, since the institution will need your divorce decree in hand.

     DONE on _____!

5.   **Calendar yourself to follow up in about six weeks to verify your beneficiary designation has been updated.**

NEXT PAGE

Check one:

_____   I finished this step on _____(date)_____ and marked "Day 11" on my calendar.

_____   This step did not apply to me because _____

_____

_____.

STOP – Day 11 is complete. Good work!

Day 12: Change Beneficiaries on Life Insurance Policies

If you owe your former spouse money, it is not unusual for you to be required to maintain life insurance in her favor. Maybe you owe child support or alimony for some period of time. Or perhaps part of your property settlement required you to make regular payments or a balloon payment, or both. If your divorce decree or agreement requires you to maintain life insurance in favor of your former spouse and/or your children, then you must do so, and you risk contempt sanctions if you fail to maintain sufficient coverage. Here's what you should do:

1. **If you don't have coverage, go apply for coverage.** Probably the best place to start is with your auto, home, or renter's insurance provider, as you can often receive discounts for maintaining multiple policies. That said, it is still worth shopping around for the best deal you can find. Try and find an independent broker with access to multiple carriers, as he or she will be able to essentially shop multiple carriers at once to try and find you the best deal for what you need.

   You should also, if at all possible, try to find and consider using an insurance agent who specializes in *only* life insurance. Many agents will sell life insurance as part of an array of products which includes auto, home, and other "property-and-casualty" insurance. While these agents would generally not intentionally lead you astray, there are a number of subtle, yet significant differences between life insurance and other types of insurance, and an agent who does not specialize may not be fully aware of how those differences can affect you or should apply to your individual situation.

   DONE on _____!

2. **If you do have coverage, contact your agent and verify your beneficiary designation.** If it is your former spouse, and should continue to be your former spouse, then you're all set. Ask your agent for proof of coverage and skip to step 5. But if the beneficiaries should be your former spouse *and your children*, then you may need to do some paperwork.

   If your divorce decree or agreement provides that your children are to be beneficiaries, and they are minors, you should probably not designate them directly. Instead, a better practice would be to designate your former spouse as guardian or trustee for the children (especially if your divorce agreement requires you to designate your former spouse in this manner), and/or designate the more general "guardian of the children" as an alternative or secondary beneficiary if your former spouse predeceases the children.

You might also consider designating a living trust or some other type of trust which benefits the children as the beneficiary of your life insurance proceeds. Whether this is a good option for you is beyond the scope of this book. Consult a qualified estate-planning attorney for guidance on how to do this, and be sure whatever you do complies with what is required by your divorce agreement.

DONE on _____!

3. **If necessary, obtain the necessary forms to change your beneficiaries and fill them out.** You will probably need identifying information about the new beneficiaries, such as Social Security numbers and/or dates of birth. Obtain those from your former spouse if necessary; your divorce decree or agreement probably obligates her to cooperate, and of course she has an incentive to do so.

Note that in some cases, you can designate "partial beneficiaries". For instance, let's say you are divorced but have no children; you have nieces and nephews you'd like to provide for if you pass away; you have an obligation to provide $250,000 in coverage to your former spouse; and you have a $1,000,000 policy already in force. You should be able to designate $250,000 in coverage for your former spouse and have your nieces and nephews designated as beneficiaries for the rest of the policy. Your agent should be able to help you set this up.

DONE on _____!

4. **Forward the appropriate paperwork to your agent and ask him/her to provide you with proof of coverage once the beneficiaries have been changed.**

DONE on _____!

5. **Provide proof of coverage to your former spouse.** Make sure you can prove delivery of this information, just in case you need it later.

DONE on _____!

6. **Put a note on your calendar eleven months from now to ask your agent for updated proof of coverage.** Many divorce decrees/agreements obligate you to provide proof of coverage on an annual basis. While you could probably make your former spouse ask you first, you should be proactive in this regard.

DONE on _____!

7. **Put another note on your calendar when you expect your obligation to provide life insurance coverage to your former spouse under the divorce decree/agreement will expire.** At that point, you will be able to go through the above process to designate whomever you want as the new beneficiary of your life insurance coverage.

DONE on _____!

If you don't have a continuing court-ordered obligation to continue to provide life insurance coverage for your former spouse, then you should contact your agent right away, obtain the necessary forms, fill them out with your new beneficiary information, and return them to your agent as soon as possible. That way you can ensure the proceeds of your policy go to the person(s) whom you designate, rather than your former spouse.

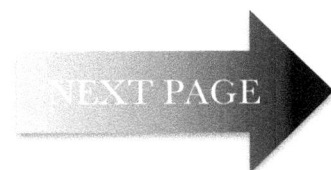

NEXT PAGE

Check one:

_____   I finished this step on _____(date)_____ and marked
                "Day 12" on my calendar.

_____   This step did not apply to me because _____

_____

_____.

STOP – Day 12 is complete. Good work!

Day 13: Get Your QDROs Done

What's a "QDRO", you might ask? It stands for "qualified domestic relations order", which is a mouthful, so often we will abbreviate that phrase "QDRO", commonly pronounced "QUA-dro". It is a special type of court order that is used to transfer part of a "qualified" retirement plan (typically, a 401(k), a 403(b), or similar type of account) from one former spouse (i.e, the account-holder) to the other former spouse.

QDROs are interesting animals. Perhaps most notably, the retirement plan itself is free to disregard the QDRO – notwithstanding that it is a court order – if the plan determines the QDRO does not meet the plan requirements. For that reason, I always recommend the plan should be involved in the drafting process as early as possible.

At this point I should note that you should probably hire an attorney to help you with this step. You *can* do this part yourself, and I will explain how, but this is one of those situations where qualified counsel can make this a lot easier for you and help you avoid certain pitfalls. If your divorce lawyer won't handle this for you, ask him for a referral to one who will.

That said, here's the process I recommend:

1. **You'll need a copy of the most recent retirement statement for the account from which the transfer will be initiated that you can find, and a certified copy of your divorce decree.**

    DONE on _____!

2. **If you don't already have one, open an Individual Retirement Account ("IRA") where the funds transferred from your former spouse's plan will be deposited.** A financial planner's assistance is highly recommended for this step. In general, you will probably be better off finding a fee-based planner instead of a commission-based planner, especially if you do not already have much in the way of retirement planning experience. The reason is that a fee-based planner generally has less of an incentive to try and steer you toward or away from a particular investment vehicle. [See Day 23 for more information on this topic.]

One alternative, if you do not have and do not want your own IRA, might be to open your own account with your former spouse's plan. This is certainly convenient for the plan (in most cases), but note that you may not be able to move the funds somewhere else later if you change your mind. Be sure you understand the pros and cons of having an account with your former spouse's plan – or any other institution – before you open such an account.

DONE on _____!

3. **Call the plan and track down the account representative assigned to your former spouse's account.** Be prepared to spend a fair amount of time on the phone. Once you track this person down, make sure you get his/her direct dial, an email address, and a physical address (not a P.O. Box).

DONE on _____!

4. **Ask the account rep to email you their form QDRO, if they have one, or the checklist they use when they receive a new QDRO, if they don't.** Larger plans have their own forms and tend to adopt a take-it-or-leave-it attitude about their form. If the plan does not have its own form, the account rep should at least be able to tell you what process they use to confirm a QDRO drafted by someone else will be accepted by the plan.

DONE on _____!

5. **Draft a proposed QDRO.** If the plan has its own, use that. If not, I've included a form that should work in most cases in Appendix B. Try and follow the checklist the plan gives you (if they give you one) to make sure everything the plan wants to be included makes its way into your proposed QDRO.

DONE on _____!

6. **Send your proposed QDRO to the plan with a written request that they respond to confirm the QDRO will be acceptable to the plan if entered in its current form.** You may have to follow up with the account rep a couple of times before you have written confirmation, but it's well worth it, just to be sure the plan won't renege on you later.

       DONE on _____!

7. **Once you have confirmation from the plan that the form of the QDRO is acceptable, forward it to the Court with a cover letter requesting it be entered.** You may want to include a copy of your divorce decree and/or agreement which indicates the court has the authority to enter the QDRO, and the good news is that these do not have to be certified copies (since the court can take judicial notice of its own orders). You generally do not need to file a new lawsuit or have a case pending, and if you demonstrate to the court that the QDRO is merely a formality to effectuate a transfer that was already made in the divorce decree/agreement, you don't even necessarily need to copy your former spouse – although you should, and it's good form if you do.

       DONE on _____!

8. **Once the QDRO has been entered by the Court, forward a certified copy of it to the plan.** A courier service such as FedEx is recommended for this step, so that you can prove delivery later.

       DONE on _____!

9. **Follow up with the account rep to ensure the funds are transferred as quickly and smoothly as possible.** The plan *should* give you no trouble at all about whether it will accept the plan, since you involved it in the drafting process and hopefully obtained written confirmation that your proposed QDRO was acceptable.

NEXT PAGE

Check one:

_____ **I finished this step on** _____(date)_____ **and marked "Day 13" on my calendar.**

_____ **This step did not apply to me because** _____

_____

_____.

STOP – Day 13 is complete. Good work!

Day 14: Get Health Insurance

If you were covered under your former spouse's health insurance plan, you lost coverage effective the day your divorce decree was entered. Coverage may be available under the federal COBRA law, but it will likely be very expensive. If you have no other choice, though, coverage under COBRA is almost certainly better than no coverage at all, since there are tax penalties for failing to carry health insurance.

There are many options available to you. If you work, you may have employer-provided coverage available. Coverage under the federal Affordable Care Act (a/k/a "Obamacare") may be available to you. Or, you could buy coverage in the private marketplace. I would strongly recommend you obtain help from someone with expertise in this arena, as it will be extremely difficult and time-consuming for you to try and sort all this out on your own.

My recommendation is that you contact an independent broker and have him/her help you. An agent with a particular agency (a so-called "captive" agent) is, of course, incentivized – if not outright forced – to offer you only products available through that agency. An independent broker, on the other hand, can effectively shop your coverage among multiple carriers in an effort to find you the best possible coverage at the lowest available rate.

At a minimum, you should ensure you have basic medical coverage. Consider adding dental, vision, and other specialized coverages, if you can afford them. Again, your broker is best-suited to help you find the right coverages for your needs.

NEXT PAGE

Check one:

_____   I finished this step on _____(date)_____ and marked "Day 14" on my calendar.

_____   This step did not apply to me because _____

_____

_____.

STOP – Day 14 is complete. Good work!

Day 15: Get Life Insurance

On Day 12, you looked at changing your beneficiaries on any life insurance policies you currently have in force. If you don't have life insurance, though, you should consider securing coverage in some amount as soon as you can.

There are a host of reasons why you should consider life insurance. The most obvious for most people is that they have kids or other dependents, for whom some financial security should be provided. Alternatively, maybe you have an asset – most commonly, a home – that needs to be protected; a life insurance policy could provide enough cash to pay off a mortgage and keep the house from being lost to the bank in the event the person paying the mortgage (i.e., you) dies and stops paying. Another reason might be to ensure there is enough cash available to pay off a loan that will survive your death and create a claim against your estate – a private student loan is a good example.

Speaking very generally, there are two types of insurance – "permanent" and "term". A permanent policy is designed to provide coverage for your entire life no matter how long you live, and generally it builds up cash value over time. A term policy, on the other hand, provides coverage for a defined period of time, and if the insured does not die within that period of time, the policy terminates without paying. Permanent policies, in general, are substantially more expensive than term policies, since they do not expire during your lifetime.

As with health insurance (see Day 14), you should consider finding an independent broker, ideally one who specializes in life insurance products specifically (see Day 12). You should also talk with your homeowner's, renter's, and/or automobile insurance agents, as adding life insurance coverage may make your pre-existing other coverages cheaper through the use of multiple-policy discounts.

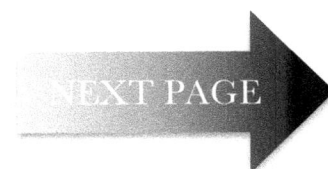

NEXT PAGE

Check one:

_____   **I finished this step on _____(date)_____ and marked "Day 15" on my calendar.**

_____   **This step did not apply to me because _____**

_____

_____.

STOP – Day 15 is complete. Good work!

Day 16: Get Umbrella Insurance

At this point you should have all your "normal" insurance coverages in place – typically automobile and home (either homeowner's or renter's). So if something happens and you're sued, you're covered. Right?

Typically auto and home insurance policies provide coverage up to a certain limit. For an auto insurance policy, most people opt for coverage of $50,000 or $100,000 (and you should consider increasing your coverage – it's probably not that much more expensive). And if you are involved in a low-speed "fender bender", that coverage is probably more than sufficient anyway. But what if you're involved in something far more serious – such as a car wreck where the other driver is left a quadriplegic?

Umbrella coverage can provide substantial extra coverage – typically $1-2 million or more – for just a couple hundred bucks a year. You may have to have higher auto and/or homeowner's coverages to be eligible for umbrella coverage, but usually the added coverage involves relatively little added expense, and it can be well worthwhile to protect your assets. Increased coverage limits and umbrella policies can save you from bankruptcy, as a catastrophic injury may make you the defendant in a lawsuit where the plaintiff is suing you for damages that exceed your entire net worth.

Once again, you can shop around, although given the low premium amount, it may not benefit you all that much to spend a lot of time on this. My suggestion is that you contact the agent who has your auto and/or home coverage and ask about adding an umbrella policy. Be sure to ask whether a multiple policy discount on your other coverage might be available if you add an umbrella policy, which will often mitigate or entirely offset the increased premiums you may have incurred on your other policies.

NEXT PAGE

Check one:

_____   **I finished this step on** ____(date)____ **and marked "Day 16" on my calendar.**

_____   **This step did not apply to me because** _____

_____

_____.

STOP – Day 16 is complete. Good work!

Day 17: Update Your Estate Plan

Today's project can be as simple or as complicated as you want to make it. At a bare minimum, you should have a new will drawn up. Even if you had a will previously, I do not recommend a "codicil" (i.e., a formal supplement to a previously published will that explains, modifies, or revokes some or all of the will) or other amendment. Instead, I suggest you completely republish a brand new will that contains no mention of your former spouse as a beneficiary, even if you don't change anything else.

There are potentially a host of other components of a good estate plan that you might consider. Two relatively simple and (usually) inexpensive options are a financial (or "durable") power of attorney and a health care power of attorney (and/or a so-called "living will", a/k/a an advance medical directive). The former instrument will allow you to name someone who is empowered to make decisions and take actions in your name with respect to your finances. For instance, your attorney-in-fact could sign checks to pay your bills if you are unavailable or incapacitated. The latter instrument(s) can empower someone to make health care and end-of-life decisions for you when you are incapable of making such decisions yourself. Again, even if you already have these instruments in place, it is worth republishing them to ensure your former spouse is not empowered to act for you under any circumstances.

There are as many options and vehicles for estate planning as there are people. For instance, depending on the size and/or complexity of the estate, you may also consider creating one or more trusts. Even if your estate is relatively modest and your beneficiary designations are fairly straight-forward, I recommend you contact qualified counsel who has experience drafting estate plans. Often this is a team effort potentially involving a financial planner, a CPA, insurance agent(s), retirement plan administrator(s), and possibly others. Though the cost is not negligible, it is probably not as much as you think. No matter what, it is far cheaper than getting it wrong or doing nothing.

I feel very strongly about this, even if finances are an issue for you. If you truly cannot afford to hire an estate planning attorney, see if your divorce attorney will provide this service for you at a discount rate. If pre-paid legal services are an available benefit of your employment, consider signing up so they will draft a low-cost will for you. There are also online services that may provide you a cost-effective solution.

The bottom line is – you should have this taken care of one way or another. If you don't have a will, the State will have one for you, i.e., the State will make decisions about your money, your property, and even your children (if they are not adults), and those decisions may not be the ones you would have made. This is one instance in which having a badly done will is probably better than having no will at all. You can (and should) always plan to revisit this with more qualified counsel later, when your finances have improved.

Check one:

_____ **I finished this step on _____(date)_____ and marked "Day 17" on my calendar.**

_____ **This step did not apply to me because _____**

_____

_____.

STOP – Day 17 is complete. Good work!

Day 18: Refinance Your Mortgage or Sign a New Lease

If you were awarded the marital residence (or any other real estate) in your divorce, you probably need to make sure your former spouse is no longer on the debt associated with it. If you are buying, that means refinancing your mortgage. If you are renting, that means amending your lease.

If the house was secured by a mortgage in joint names, you will need to refinance the mortgage if you can't pay it off. The easiest thing to do is probably to ask your current lender, but it is probably worth shopping around a bit for the best rate you can find. Before you do, make sure you know the answers to the following questions (ideally, have them typed out so you can quickly email them to a potential lender or broker):

➤ What is your current total monthly payment?

_____

➤ Does your payment include your taxes and insurance?

_____

➤ What is the cost of your annual property taxes and homeowners insurance?

_____

➤ How much do you owe on your existing mortgage?

_____

➤ When did you take out your existing mortgage?

_____

➤ Do you know if it's a Fannie Mae, Freddie Mac, or FHA insured loan?

_____

➤ What are your overall goals in refinancing your mortgage (remove former spouse's name, shorten term, lower rate, lower payment, etc.)?

_____

➤ At what value do you think your home will appraise?

_____

➤ What is your property's address?

_____

If, on the other hand, you were renting, you will want to notify your landlord (if you haven't already) that your former spouse has moved out and that he is no longer a responsible party on the lease. At a minimum, you will probably want your landlord to prepare an amendment to your lease to that effect. However, you may also want to see if your landlord will negotiate a new lease, particularly if you intend to stay long-term. Your landlord may be willing to make certain concessions to you in exchange for the security of a longer-term tenant.

Check one:

_____ **I finished this step on _____(date)_____ and marked "Day 18" on my calendar.**

_____ **This step did not apply to me because _____**

_____

_____.

STOP – Day 18 is complete. Good work!

Day 19: Retitle Your House

Yesterday, you looked at refinancing the mortgage on real property awarded to you (e.g., the former marital residence). Once your former spouse is no longer responsible to the lender for the debt against your house, the house itself should be awarded outright to you, and the former spouse's name should come off the deed. Alternatively, if you happen to own the house outright, you will also want to be sure the title to the house is transferred to your sole name. Either way, this is particularly important if you and your former spouse held the property as "joint tenants with right of survivorship" – what this means is that if you die, your former spouse receives the entire property, entirely outside your probate estate.

Fortunately, this is usually a pretty easy process. You may have to engage an attorney or other qualified real estate professional to help you. However, if you live in a state where this is not required, you don't have to refinance your mortgage, and you don't have any other liens against the property, you may be able to handle this project on your own. Here's the process:

1. **Find a copy of the deed to your house.** It's probably a "warranty deed" with yourself and your former spouse named as "grantees".

    DONE on _____!

2. **Find a sample form.** Do an internet search for "sample form quit claim deed [STATE]" to find the form you need for your state.

    DONE on _____!

3. **Fill out the form for your house.** You will probably need the "legal description", also known as a "metes-and-bounds description", which you may be able to attach as an exhibit. The "grantor" will probably be you and your former spouse as joint tenants – to be safe, copy the same verbiage used on your warranty deed word-for-word. The "grantee" will be you, and you alone.

    DONE on _____!

4.   **Make sure to include signature blocks for both grantors, i.e., both you and your former spouse.** You will both need to sign, even though you are also the "grantee".

   DONE on _____!

5.   **Have the quit-claim deed fully executed.** Make sure you know how many witnesses you need. The witnesses should be adults (over 18 years old) who are not related by blood or marriage to either you or your former spouse. You will probably also need a Notary Public, who should not be related by blood or marriage to either you, your former spouse, or any of the witnesses.

   DONE on _____!

6.   **Have the original quit-claim deed recorded against your property.** Generally a local government (usually the county) will maintain a registry of instruments concerning real property, so that the title to any parcel of real estate located within a given government's territory can be traced. There will be a recording process whereby the original instrument (not a copy) will be recorded in that registry so that it will be included in a title search on that property. Typically you will pay a nominal fee for this service, but the transfer of title will often be considered incomplete under the law until you take this step.

   DONE on _____!

7.   **When you get the recorded quit-claim deed back, put it in a safe place.** You should generally keep it with your other important papers, especially the actual deed to your house.

   DONE on _____!

A note of caution: in some states, an instrument of conveyance of real property – such as a deed conveying a house from two former spouses to one of the former spouses, removing the other's name from the title – must be prepared by an attorney. In those states, if you are not a lawyer and try to prepare this instrument yourself, you may be guilty of "unauthorized practice of law", for which there may be potential criminal penalties. If you live in such a state, then you have to engage a lawyer to handle this for you. If you're not sure, hiring a lawyer is the safest course of action.

Check one:

_____   **I finished this step on** _____(date)_____ **and marked "Day 19" on my calendar.**

_____   **This step did not apply to me because** _____

_____

_____.

STOP – Day 19 is complete. Good work!

Day 20: Retitle Your Car

As with real property awarded to you, personal property awarded to you –
notably, your car and other vehicles (motorcycles, boats, RV's, trailers, etc.)
– should be retitled so that your former spouse's name is removed from the
title to the property. Usually, this is a fairly simple process:

1. **Find the original title certificate to your vehicle.** If you cannot
   locate the original title certificate, you'll have to replace it. Do an
   internet search for "replacing lost car title [STATE]" and follow
   whatever directions you find. The *www.dmv.org* web site is also a good
   resource, no matter where you live.

    DONE on _____!

2. **Have your spouse sign the title over to you on the original
   title certificate.**

    DONE on _____!

3. **Have the issuing authority (generally, the "department of
   motor vehicles" or "department of driver services") re-
   issue the title certificate.**

    DONE on _____!

4. **When you receive the re-issued title certificate, keep it with
   your other important papers.**

NEXT PAGE

Check one:

_____   **I finished this step on** _____(date)_____ **and marked "Day 20" on my calendar.**

_____   **This step did not apply to me because** _____

_____

_____.

STOP – Day 20 is complete. Good work!

PAUSE AND REFLECT

You've been at it for about three weeks, and you're two-thirds of the way done. Take a moment and reflect on what you've been able to accomplish in the last ten days:

➤ You have changed the beneficiaries on your retirement accounts and life insurance policies.

➤ You have initiated the transfers to or from your retirement accounts that are required by your divorce decree or agreement.

➤ You have health, life, and umbrella insurance.

➤ You have an updated estate plan.

➤ You refinanced your mortgage or signed a new lease.

➤ You retitled your house and all your vehicles.

That's a lot of stuff, and you should be proud! Before you keep going, though, you should take a moment and reflect. How do you feel? Take 60 seconds and write down how you're feeling about this process so far. Set a timer if you have to. Again, don't think, just write. Ready? GO!

_____

_____

_____

NOW you can keep going. Good work!

Day 21: Update ALL Your Insurance

If you've been diligently following along to this point, you've already done the following:

➤ You obtained life insurance and/or updated your life insurance beneficiaries. [Day 12, Day 15]

➤ You obtained health insurance. [Day 14]

➤ You verified and may have increased your homeowner's, renter's, and/or automobile insurance coverage limits, and you may have obtained umbrella insurance. [Day 16]

➤ You refinanced your mortgage and retitled your house. [Day 18, Day 19]

➤ You retitled your car. [Day 20]

At this point, it's time to go back and make sure all of your insurance is correct.

1. **Update your homeowner's, renter's, and/or automobile insurance now that your former spouse is no longer on the mortgage, lease, and/or title to your property.**

    DONE on _____!

2. **Consider obtaining or updating other insurance coverages as your finances allow.** Areas to consider include the following:

    ➤ umbrella coverage [see Day 16]

    ➤ short-term disability coverage

    ➤ long-term care

    ➤ critical illness protection

    ➤ supplemental insurance (to provide you with personal cash flow when you are unable to work)

NEXT PAGE

Check one:

_____   **I finished this step on** _____(date)_____ **and marked "Day 21" on my calendar.**

_____   **This step did not apply to me because** _____

_____

_____.

STOP – Day 21 is complete. Good work!

Day 22: Get a Tax Accountant

Chances are, you are not a tax accountant. Even if you are, you probably shouldn't do your own taxes, simply because you are not objective.

You may not need a tax accountant; "do-it-yourself" software like TurboTax or a tax preparation service like H&R Block might work for you just fine. But if any of the following apply, you should strongly consider hiring a tax accountant:

➤ Your income is reasonably high (over $120,000/year).

➤ You own an interest in a small business – either as a sole owner, a partner, or a shareholder/stakeholder.

➤ You are *not* subject to the Alternative Minimum Tax ("AMT"), or you aren't sure.

➤ You receive income from outside the United States.

➤ You own rental properties or any other investment from which you derive significant income.

➤ You are selling, have sold, or are considering selling real estate and/or an interest in a business.

➤ Your estate plan is anything more complicated than "leave all my money to ___".

➤ You expect a substantial capital tax gain.

➤ You have a child in college.

➤ You use a tax preparer, and the preparer recommends you consult an accountant. (A good preparer will make this recommendation without hesitation if the circumstances suggest to him that this would be a good idea for you.)

A good tax accountant will become a vital advisor for you for the long term. Don't wait until right before tax day. Also, I recommend you hire a tax *accountant* – someone who can help you *plan* – and not merely a tax *preparer*. This person is probably a CPA, preferably with significant experience.

NEXT PAGE ➤

Check one:

_____ **I finished this step on _____(date)_____ and marked "Day 22" on my calendar.**

_____ **This step did not apply to me because _____**

_____

_____.

STOP – Day 22 is complete. Good work!

Day 23: Get a Financial Planner

Yesterday's task was to find a tax accountant. Today, you should look for a financial planner, for many of the same reasons. First and foremost, you are probably not a financial planner. In addition, you may never have done any of your own financial planning. Even if you are a financial planner and have done much of your own planning, it is strongly recommended that you find a planner anyway, if for no other reason than for a "sanity check", i.e., to have a second set of eyes on your own plan. Other reasons to hire a financial planner include:

➤ If you and your former spouse had a planner together, you should find someone else, especially if your former spouse is sticking with your old planner.

➤ If you received a substantial amount of retirement and/or other financial assets (stocks, bonds, mutual funds, etc.) in the divorce, you need a financial planner, especially if you have no experience managing such assets.

➤ If you have more than three retirement/financial accounts, you need a financial planner to make sure it's all part of a coherent plan.

If you think about it, you have taken several steps already toward a viable long-term financial "plan":

➤ You did some credit repair. [Day 3, Day 10]

➤ You looked at your retirement accounts [Day 11] and life insurance coverage [Day 12] to make sure your beneficiaries are correct.

➤ You made sure you had life [Day 15] and umbrella [Day 16] insurance coverage.

➤ You updated your estate plan. [Day 17]

Arguably, the biggest value a financial planner can add is to bring a sense of cohesion to whatever you're currently doing. Think for a moment about whether you really have *goals* for your finances – or do you just have *hopes*? A financial planner can take your vague hopes and help you figure out how to turn them into realistic goals.

One thing to watch out for when choosing a financial planner is to see how independent he is. If he works for a financial institution, keep in mind that he has an incentive to steer you toward products offered by that institution, and he may not have access to products that are generally available elsewhere. An independent planner, on the other hand, is not beholden to a particular vendor. As a result, he is often more capable of steering you toward products and plans that work best for your specific needs.

Another consideration when choosing a financial planner is whether his compensation is "fee-based" or "commission-based". In general, if you have not had much (or any) experience with financial planners, you should try to find a fee-based planner. The reason is that commission-based planners are incentivized to sell particular products or plans – that's how they make their money. A fee-based planner, on the other hand, is generally paid by the hour no matter what you end up doing with him. As a result, his advice tends to be more objective.

Like your tax accountant and your attorney, your financial planner should become one of your trusted advisors over the long term. Be very careful when evaluating financial planners – treat it like a job interview, including checking experience and following up with current clients.

Check one:

_____ **I finished this step on _____(date)_____ and marked "Day 23" on my calendar.**

_____ **This step did not apply to me because _____**

_____

_____.

STOP – Day 23 is complete. Good work!

Day 24: Buy a Cross-Cut Shredder and Put It to Work

You probably have accumulated a whole pile of documents that have some highly sensitive information on them, such as your birthday, your social security number, medical information, and so on. These kinds of documents are invaluable to an identity thief. If you don't need to keep any of that stuff, it's time to get rid of it – but make sure you do so safely and securely.

If you don't have a cross-cut shredder, buy one. They are not terribly expensive; you should be able to get a serviceable model, brand new, for under $100. Make sure you don't buy a "strip-cut" shredder – in this day and age, identity thieves can actually piece strip-shredded documents back together with relatively little difficulty. A cross-cut or "micro-cut" shredder is much more secure.

If you have documents you want to keep "just in case", you can scan them and store them digitally, ideally in an encrypted format of some kind. How to do that is beyond the scope of this book. The point is, even if you do this, make sure you securely destroy the paper versions once you're finished.

Here's a list of what you should consider shredding:

➤ any document listing your (or your children's) birth dates, Social Security numbers, a password or "PIN" (even if you have never used it)

➤ any document relating to a closed or expired account (bank account, credit cards, etc.)

➤ anything with your signature on it that you don't need to keep for some other reason

➤ anything you would carry in your wallet but which has expired or been cancelled (driver's license, military ID, credit card, etc.)

➤ pay stubs

➤ retirement account statements

➤ bank and credit card statements

➤ bank "starter" checks (once you have your real checks, of course), duplicate or cancelled checks, and credit card "convenience" checks

- ➤ monthly bills

- ➤ any documents showing travel arrangements

- ➤ "pre-approved" credit card offers and similar junk mail – get in the habit of shredding these every time you bring in the mail

- ➤ employment contracts and other records from past jobs – make sure there aren't obligations on either you or your former employer which are still in force

- ➤ title documents, mortgage paperwork, rental agreements, appraisals, and insurance documents from property you no longer own or rent

- ➤ car titles, loan documents, and insurance documents for vehicles you no longer own or lease

- ➤ school transcripts

- ➤ tax returns over seven years old

- ➤ if your name changed, anything with your old name that you don't need to keep for some other reason (e.g., tax returns that are less than seven years old)

Note that if any of the documents on this list relate to assets which carry tax implications – for instance, rental properties, vehicles used for business purposes, or equipment for which you claimed depreciation expenses – you should keep those documents for at least seven years after you dispose of the asset.

If you have a lot of stuff to shred at once, you might even consider hiring someone to do it. A trustworthy vendor might shred a dozen boxes of stuff for a couple hundred bucks, and it will be securely destroyed right in your driveway. Even if you choose that option, buy a shredder anyway so you can destroy documents on the above list as they arrive in your home from now on.

NEXT PAGE

Check one:

_____   **I finished this step on** _____(date)_____ **and marked "Day 24" on my calendar.**

_____   **This step did not apply to me because** _____

_____

_____.

STOP – Day 24 is complete. Good work!

Day 25: Get a Safe Deposit Box or Personal Fireproof Safe

Yesterday, you purged a whole bunch of sensitive documents that you don't need to keep any more. Chances are, however, there are at least a few documents that you do need to keep, at least for awhile. So today's goal is to make sure you have a safe place to keep them.

One easy option might be to get a safe deposit box at your bank. Though not terribly expensive in most cases, there is a monthly fee, although some banks might offer you a safe deposit box for free as a benefit of having your account(s) there. It can also be somewhat inconvenient if you need documents in the bank, since you can only get them by driving to your bank during banking hours. On the other hand, the bank's security is almost certainly better than yours, so your documents are probably better protected at the bank than in your home.

Alternatively, you can buy a home safe. There are basically three things a home safe can protect your documents from – fire, burglary, and water. Fire protection is probably your number one concern. Burglary protection is usually lower on the list, especially if you are only going to store documents. However, if you are considering storing other valuables (jewelry, for instance), you may want to keep this in mind. As for water protection, you should be less concerned about whether your home is likely to flood and more concerned about the damage that can be done by leaky plumbing, sprinklers, and firefighters.

You can buy a good fire box for $50.00 or less, or a decent safe for probably $200 or so. Take a moment to consider where to locate it within your home. Try to avoid obvious areas such as the master bedroom or the home office. As for what you may want to keep in it:

➤   birth and death certificates

➤   your will, powers of attorney, and other estate-planning documents

➤   life insurance policies (until they expire)

➤   savings bonds, stock certificates, and other financial instruments

➤   certified copies of your divorce paperwork [see Day 26]

➤   anything from yesterday's list that you decided to save

Check one:

_____ I finished this step on _____(date)_____ and marked "Day 25" on my calendar.

_____ This step did not apply to me because _____

_____

_____.

STOP – Day 25 is complete. Good work!

Day 26: Get Extra Certified Copies of Important Documents

Sometimes you need certified copies of your divorce decree, settlement agreement, parenting or custodial arrangement, and other papers filed in your divorce case. A "certified" copy is different from a regular copy in that the clerk of the court has put a special stamp and certification on the copy. There is almost always a small fee for the certification (in addition to copy costs you are likely to be charged).

It's a good idea to keep one certified copy on hand, just in case you need it. Obtaining certified copies is as simple as going to the courthouse and asking the clerk of court for them. Some things to keep in mind:

➤ You will need the "style" of your case (e.g., "John Doe v. Jane Doe" and the case number).

➤ You should bring a regular copy of the documents you want, to make sure you get copies of the correct documents.

➤ You should bring cash if you can; most court clerks will not take a personal check.

➤ You may be able to receive certified copies by mail; call the clerk's office to see if this is a possibility.

Keep your certified copies in a safe place. If you have a safe deposit box or home safe [see Day 25], keep them in there.

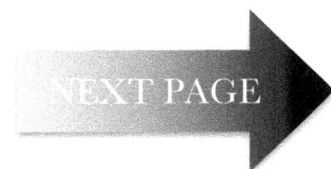

NEXT PAGE

Check one:

_____   I finished this step on _____(date)_____ and marked
             "Day 26" on my calendar.

_____   This step did not apply to me because _____

_____

_____.

STOP – Day 26 is complete. Good work!

Day 27: Get Proof of Life Insurance from Your Spouse

If your former spouse owes you child support and/or alimony, he may have an obligation to provide life insurance coverage in your favor until his support obligations have been fulfilled. If he has not already provided you with proof of coverage, go ahead and ask him to do so. A sample letter has been provided in Appendix B.

You should specifically ask for the "declaration page". The declaration page contains most of the information you need (name of the insured, amount and type of coverage, policy number, name and address of the insurer) but generally does not identify the beneficiaries. Therefore, you will also need the portion of the insurance policy which designates the beneficiaries. Often this is done in the insurance application, but if beneficiaries are changed on a policy in force, there will be a subsequent beneficiary designation page.

Once you have obtained this information, keep it in a safe place – ideally, in your safe deposit box or home safe [see Day 25]. You should also put a note on your calendar for one year from now to ask for updated proof of coverage.

Check one:

_____ **I finished this step on** _____(date)_____ **and marked "Day 27" on my calendar.**

_____ **This step did not apply to me because** _____

_____

_____.

STOP – Day 27 is complete. Good work!

Day 28: Go Through Every Room in Your Home

You've probably been separated for months or years, and you've been divorced for several weeks. Your former spouse has long since moved out, and hopefully he has taken everything with him. Today's exercise is designed to help you make sure your former spouse's belongings have been fully purged from your home.

Find a box or a laundry basket and start systematically moving through every room in your house, condo, or apartment. Open closets and look behind stuff. Open every drawer and rummage through it. Look under and behind beds and other furniture. If you find something that belongs to your former spouse, put it in the box. **Don't stop when you find something**; just put it in the box and keep going until you've gone through every room.

Once you've been through every room, then you can go through the box and decide what to do with what you've found. If it's trash or something you're absolutely sure he won't want, throw it away or give it away. But if you have any question, keep it for now. Make a list of everything you keep and ask him if he wants it back. You should also tell him that if he doesn't make arrangements to pick up whatever he wants back by a certain day, then you're going to dispose of it. Make sure you pick a reasonable deadline – a couple of weeks at the very minimum.

Put it all in a box and write the deadline date on the outside with a marker. Put that date on your calendar and put the box somewhere out of your way. Once the deadline date comes and goes, get the box back out and throw away or give away everything in it.

Your home is now all yours again.

NEXT PAGE

Check one:

_____   **I finished this step on** _____(date)_____ **and marked "Day 28" on my calendar.**

_____   **This step did not apply to me because** _____

_____

_____.

STOP – Day 28 is complete. Good work!

Day 29: Put Together a Basic Debt Payoff Plan

One of the most common causes of divorce is money issues. Chances are good you have some debt, either as a result of your divorce or in connection with it (for instance, you may have incurred debt to set up a new household after separating from your former spouse). Today's exercise will involve re-evaluating your debt in the context of your overall financial circumstances, and figuring out what it will take for you to eliminate it for good. There are many ways to tackle this problem, but here's a good way to get started:

1. **Make a list of every single debt you have.** Find the most recent statement for each one you can and write down the name and phone number of the creditor, the total amount currently due, the interest rate, the amount of your minimum payment, and the amount that is past due, if any. You can do this by hand or use a computer, your choice.

   DONE on _____!

2. **Sort the list according to the total amount currently due, listing the smallest balance first.**

   DONE on _____!

3. **Call every creditor and see if they will renegotiate any of your payment terms.** If you have a past-due balance, see if they will roll that into the current balance and forgive late fees, etc. If the interest rate is fairly high, see if they'll give you a lower rate or a grace period of a few months to try and catch up. While they are not obligated to do anything for you, you might be surprised at how many of your creditors will be willing to work with you once you explain that you are newly divorced and are making a conscious effort to reduce your debt. If the creditor does offer you better terms, cross out the old information and update your list as you go.

   DONE on _____!

4. **If you have the cash to do so, pay off as many of your debts as you can in a lump sum.** Do not use your emergency savings [see Day 9] or retirement accounts, but if you have other cash available – for example, maybe you received a lump sum in the divorce – consider paying off a debt. In most cases, you should only

make a substantial payment like this if you can completely pay it off. That said, if the creditor is willing to offer you more favorable terms on the balance once you have made a significant lump sum payment, then that may be worth doing. If you do pay off a debt, cross it off the list.

DONE on _____!

5. **Sort the list again according to the total amount currently due, listing the smallest balance first.** This time, also write out the minimum monthly payment for each one.

DONE on _____!

6. **If you have multiple credit cards, go through the list and figure out which credit card you have had the longest.** Make a special note of that one.

DONE on _____!

7. **Figure out how much you need every month to pay your needed bills.** In addition to utilities, groceries, etc., make sure you include the minimum monthly payments for all of your debts.

DONE on _____!

8. **Determine how much "discretionary" income you have after covering your regular expenses.** If your regular expenses exceed your net income, you need to find a way to make more money, cut your expenses, or both. That said, don't forget to include *all* sources of income, including support from your former spouse, if any.

DONE on _____!

9. **Commit to paying your "discretionary" income toward the debt at the top of your list, in addition to the minimum monthly payment due to that creditor, every month until that debt is paid.** By ordering the list as described above, you have figured how to pay the most money toward the smallest debt, thus retiring it the fastest. Once you have paid the balance all the way off, be sure to direct the creditor (in writing) to close the account.

There is one exception. If the debt you are focusing on aggressively eliminating is the credit card you identified in step 6, don't eliminate that debt entirely, but rather, leave a small balance (say, $100.00). The reason is that closing this card – which is your oldest credit card – will actually hurt your credit rating by shortening your credit history. The reason I recommend you don't actually pay this balance all the way down to zero ($0.00) is that you don't want the creditor to decide to close the account on its own. Instead, my recommendation is that you set up a recurring payment using this card – see Day 10 for more about this.

DONE on _____!

10. **Automate all of your other debt payments so you don't have to think about – dwell on – any of them.** You are only paying the minimum on these debts, essentially keeping them from becoming derogatory while you focus on eliminating the smallest one.

DONE on _____!

11. **When you eventually pay off a debt, commit to paying your "discretionary" income – which now includes the minimum monthly payment on the debt you just retired – toward the next debt on the list.** Be sure, however, to celebrate eliminating that one debt in some meaningful way. Go out to dinner, or take a day trip to a favorite place, whatever strikes your fancy.

DONE on _____!

The above process is a variant on the "debt snowball" method propounded by Dave Ramsey and others. The focus is on celebrating the elimination – forever – of each of your debts, one at a time, as quickly as you can wipe them out. Its primary advantages are simplicity and automation. Ideally, you can automate this process so much that the only thing you will handle manually will be paying off the top debt on the list, since the amount of "extra" that you're paying on that debt can differ month-to-month.

One final thought: if you have a substantial amount of debt, particularly unsecured debt (credit cards, medical bills, and utility payments are the most common types), without the means to retire it in the next several years, you may want to consider filing for bankruptcy protection. Many people have strong negative feelings about filing for bankruptcy. However, if you truly are so crushed by debt that you have no realistic chance of getting out from under it any time soon, it is an option that you owe it to yourself to consider. At the very least, you should consult with qualified bankruptcy counsel; just because you meet with an attorney for an hour and ask a bunch of questions doesn't mean you have to actually go through with a bankruptcy filing.

Check one:

_____   **I finished this step on _____(date)_____ and marked "Day 29" on my calendar.**

_____   **This step did not apply to me because _____**

_____

_____.

STOP – Day 29 is complete. Good work!

Day 30: Review Your Divorce Paperwork, One More Time

By now you are probably so sick of even thinking about your divorce, the thought of digging out your divorce agreement and reading through it, line by line, paragraph by paragraph, is just about the last thing you want to do. But I recommend you do it one more – hopefully one *last* – time.

➤ If there's something you're supposed to do that you haven't already done, make a note of it so you can get to work on it. If it's something you can't do yet, put it on your calendar.

➤ If there's something your former spouse is supposed to have already done that he hasn't done yet, make a note to follow up with him to do it. If you follow up and he is unresponsive, call your lawyer and have him review your options with you.

➤ If there's something your former spouse is supposed to do that isn't due yet, mark the deadline on your calendar.

➤ If you owe a support obligation to your former spouse, or your former spouse owes a support obligation to you, mark the expiration date on your calendar.

➤ If the amount of the support is supposed to change at some point before it expires, then mark the dates when you expect the support obligation to change on your calendar. One common scenario, for example, is that child support may reduce when one child graduates from high school, but will not go away entirely because there are younger children who still need support. Another common example occurs when alimony is to be paid at one rate for some period of time, then a reduced rate for a later period of time.

➤ If you are entitled to annual or other regular updates from your former spouse, or if you are required to provide annual or other updates to your former spouse, mark those deadlines on your calendar.

➤ If you are entitled to a share of your former spouse's retirement, mark his expected retirement date on your calendar, if possible.

There may be something in your divorce paperwork that you just don't understand for some reason. Or, you may have questions about something in your divorce paperwork. If that's the case, call your lawyer and have him explain it to you.

Now, put your divorce paperwork away – hopefully you don't need to refer to it any more in the near future.

Check one:

_____ **I finished this step on _____(date)_____ and marked "Day 30" on my calendar.**

_____ **This step did not apply to me because _____**

_____

_____.

STOP – Day 30 is complete. Good work!

Day 31: Celebrate!

WOW! Look what you did!

Hopefully by now you feel like you've accomplished something. If you worked all the way through this book, take it from me – you have, and that's worth celebrating! Time to break out that bottle of wine or go on that trip, or whatever else it was you planned to do when you reached this goal.

But before you do, remember back before you started, I asked you to write down how you felt going into this process. Let's do that again – take 60 seconds and write down how you're feeling about this process. Set a timer if you have to, and **DON'T CHEAT** by looking back first. Don't think, just write. Ready? GO!

_____

_____

_____

_____

_____

_____

Now, go back to page 12 and look at what you wrote when you started, and compare it to what you just wrote above. If that doesn't make you feel good about this process, I don't know what will.

Congratulations! Enjoy the rest of your post-divorce life!

Appendix A: Blank Calendar Template

You can either copy and use this as needed, or there is a customizable version of this template available at www.postdivorcecompass.com.

Month:						
Mon	**Tue**	**Wed**	**Thu**	**Fri**	**Sat**	**Sun**

Appendix B: Sample Forms and Letters

NOTE: Downloadable versions of these are available at www.postdivorcecompass.com. You are free to copy any of these forms for your personal use.

Day 2 – Income Deduction Order ("IDO")

Day 2 – Cover Letter to Send IDO to Judge

Day 2 – Notice Letter to Employer

Day 13 – Qualified Domestic Relations Order ("QDRO")

Day 13 – Cover Letter to Send QDRO to Judge

Day 27 – Letter to Former Spouse Requesting Proof of Life Insurance Coverage

Day 2 – Income Deduction Order ("IDO")

IN THE _[1]_ COURT OF _[2]_ COUNTY
STATE OF _[3]_

_[4]_,
     Plaintiff,
 	
 v.
 	
 _[5]_,
     Defendant.
	CIVIL ACTION FILE
	
	 NO. _[6]_

INCOME DEDUCTION ORDER

1. These terms, as used herein, will be defined as follows:

Obligor:	**_[7]_**
Payee:	**_[8]_**
Payee's Address:	**_[9]_**
Payor(s):	**any and every employer, future employer, or any other person, private entity, federal or state government or agency, or any unit of local government providing or administering income due to Obligor as wages, salary, bonus, commission, compensation as an independent contractor, workers compensation, unemployment compensation, disability benefits, annuity and retirement benefits, pensions, dividends, interest, royalties, trust or any other payments**

2. Payor(s) will deduct from all monies due and payable to Obligor the following amount until further order of this Court or as may otherwise be provided herein: beginning immediately, the lesser of **(a)** _[10a]_ ($_[10b]_) dollars per month (or an equivalent amount per pay period if Obligor is not paid monthly) from Obligor's gross income; or

(b) the maximum amount allowed under § 303.b of the federal Consumer Credit Protection Act, *15 U.S.C.S. § 1673(b)* (as amended).

3. Payor will make the amount deducted payable to, and forward it within two (2) business days after each payment date to Payee at Payee's Address, or to such future address provided by Payee to Payor(s) in a written, witnessed, and notarized statement requesting a change in such forwarding address. Payor(s) and Payee may agree, but are not required to agree, to have such amounts directly deposited to a bank account designated by Payee.

4. This Income Deduction Order will be effective immediately and will remain in effect until the termination and payment in full of the obligations required of Obligor by the Final Judgment and Decree of Divorce between the parties, or as is otherwise required by future order of this Court. This Order will supersede any previous income deduction order, including all prior income deduction orders already in place in the above-styled case.

5. This Income Deduction Order and all further papers required to be served by applicable law will be served upon the Obligor, Payee, and Payor(s), and any other parties and entities as required by the above statute, via regular mail.

   SO ORDERED this _____ day of _____, 20____.

                                    _____
                                    Judge of _[11]_ Court
                                    _[12]_ County, _[13]_

Notes for Income Deduction Order ("IDO"):

[1]   The type of trial court that granted your divorce. This can vary depending on your state but will probably be something like "Superior", "Circuit", or "District".

[2]   The name of the county in which your divorce was granted.

[3]   The name of the state in which your divorce was granted.

[4]   The full name of the plaintiff in the divorce case; either you or your former spouse.

[5]   The full name of the defendant in the divorce case; either you or your former spouse (whichever one of you is not the plaintiff).

[6]   The case number of your divorce case.

[7]   If you are receiving support, your former spouse is the "obligor". If you are paying support, you are the "obligor".

[8]   If your former spouse is the obligor, you are the "payee". If you are the obligor, your former spouse is the "payee".

[9]   The address where payments should be sent. Typically this is the payee's home address.

[10]   This is the exact amount of the monthly support payment, or the total of all payments if there is more than one payment (e.g., you are receiving both alimony and child support). You will write it twice – [a] in words (e.g., "one hundred fifty and no/100"), and [b] in numerals ("150.00").

[11]   Type of court; same as [1].

[12]   Name of county; same as [2].

[13]   Name of state; same as [3].

Day 2 – Cover Letter to Send IDO to Judge

_[1]_

Via First Class U.S. Mail:

_[2]_

> RE: _[3]_ v. _[4]_
> _[5]_ Court of _[6]_ County
> Case No. _[7]_
> Divorce Decree Entered _[8]_

Dear _[9]_,

I am the former spouse of _[10]_. This Court granted our divorce on _[11]_. A copy of this letter is sent to _[12]_.

Paragraph _[13]_ of our divorce decree **[14]** provides for support payments to be made by income deduction order. I have prepared a proposed income deduction order, which is enclosed for the Court's consideration. _[15]_

If it is acceptable, I would appreciate it if you would send me a *certified* copy of the entered income deduction order. I have enclosed a self-addressed stamped envelope for this purpose. Upon my receipt of the same, I will forward a regular copy to _[16]_ and send the certified copy to the payor.

Thank you for your attention to this matter. Please contact me at your convenience if you have questions or if I can further assist the Court.

Sincerely,

_[17]_

NOTES ON NEXT PAGE

Notes for Cover Letter to Send IDO to Judge

[1]   The date of the letter.

[2]   The name and address of the Judge. You would write the Judge's name as (for example) "Hon. John Smith". You should also address the letter specifically to the Judge's secretary, law clerk, or staff attorney, and not directly to the Judge.

[3]   The plaintiff's last name in the divorce case.

[4]   The defendant's last name in the divorce case.

[5]   The type of trial court that granted your divorce ("Superior", "Circuit", etc.).

[6]   The name of the county where your divorce was granted.

[7]   The case number of your divorce.

[8]   The date your divorce decree was "entered" (generally, the date on the clerk's file-stamp on your divorce decree).

[9]   The person to whom you are addressing the letter – probably *not* the Judge directly. See [2].

[10]   Your former spouse's name.

[11]   The date of your divorce; same as [8].

[12]   Your former spouse's name.

[13]   You will have to look up the paragraph number from the divorce decree or your settlement agreement that gives you the right to have an income deduction order entered.

[14]   You may have to change "our divorce decree" to something like "our settlement agreement", as appropriate.

[15]   OPTIONAL: You may have to include some additional explanatory language to show the Court that you are actually entitled to the income deduction order. For example, if you are only entitled to seek an income deduction order when a payment is missed, you should explain that a payment has come due on a particular date and was not made.

[16]   Your former spouse's name.

[17]   Your name.

Day 2 – Notice Letter to Employer

_[1]_

Via First Class U.S. Mail:

_[2]_

      RE: **_[3]_ v. _[4]_**
                _[5]_ Court of _[6]_ County
                Case No. _[7]_
                Divorce Decree Entered _[8]_

Dear _**[9]**_,

I am the former spouse of _**[10]**_. The Court entered an "income deduction order" on _**[11]**_, which requires you, as my former spouse's employer, to withhold support payments from his income and forward those payments to me. A certified copy of that income deduction order is enclosed.

Thank you for your attention to this matter. Please contact me at your convenience if you have questions, or if there is some problem in implementing the income deduction order.

                                  Sincerely,

                                _**[12]**_

NOTES ON NEXT PAGE

Notes for Notice Letter to Employer

[1]   The date of the letter.

[2]   The name and address of the employer.

[3]   The plaintiff's last name in the divorce case.

[4]   The defendant's last name in the divorce case.

[5]   The type of trial court that granted your divorce ("Superior", "Circuit", etc.).

[6]   The name of the county where your divorce was granted.

[7]   The case number of your divorce.

[8]   The date your divorce decree was "entered" (generally, the date on the clerk's file-stamp on your divorce decree).

[9]   The person to whom you are addressing the letter.

[10]   Your former spouse's name.

[11]   The date the income deduction order was entered.

[12]   Your name.

Day 13 – Qualified Domestic Relations Order ("QDRO")

IN THE _[1]_ COURT OF _[2]_ COUNTY
STATE OF _[3]_

_[4]_,
    Plaintiff,
 	
v.
 	
_[5]_,
    Defendant.
	CIVIL ACTION FILE
	
	NO. _[6]_

QUALIFIED DOMESTIC RELATIONS ORDER

This order creates and recognizes the existence of an Alternate Payee's right to receive a portion of the participant's benefits payable under an employer-sponsored defined contribution plan, which is qualified under Section 401 of the Internal Revenue Code (the "Code"). This order is intended to constitute a Qualified Domestic Relations Order ("QDRO") under Section 414(p) of the Code and Section 206(d) of the Employee Retirement Income Security Act of 1974 ("ERISA") and will be interpreted and administered in conformity with such laws. This order is entered pursuant to the authority granted under the applicable domestic relations laws of the state of _[7]_.

1. This Order applies to _[8]_ (the "Plan"). Any successor to this Plan will also be subject to the terms of this Order.

2. The name and address of the Participant are as follows:

    _[9]_

For privacy reasons, the Participant's Social Security Number and Date of Birth will be provided under separate cover rather than part of this Order, which will be public record.

3.   The person named as Alternate Payee is the former spouse of the Participant and therefore meets the requirements of the definition of Alternate Payee as set forth in Section 5 below. The name and address of the Alternate Payee are as follows:

_[10]_

For privacy reasons, the Alternate Payee's Social Security Number and Date of Birth will be provided under separate cover rather than part of this Order, which will be public record. The Alternate Payee will be responsible for notifying the Administrator in writing of any changes in his/her mailing address subsequent to the entry of this Order.

4.   Date of Marriage: **_[11]_**

Date of Divorce: **_[12]_**

5.   Definitions.

a.   Alternate Payee – The Alternate Payee is any spouse, former spouse, child or other dependent of a participant who is recognized by a domestic relations order as having a right to receive all or a portion of the benefits payable under the Plan with respect to the participant.

b.   Liquidation Date – The Liquidation Date is the date a portion of the participant's account is liquidated to allow the payment to the Alternate Payee's account under this order. An assignment as of

110

the Liquidation Date assigns a portion of the participant's current account.

    c. Plan Administrator – **_[13]_** ("Administrator") is the Plan Administrator for the Plan.

6. This Order assigns to the Alternate Payee, as equitable division of marital property, an amount equal to **_[14]_** from the Participant's Account under the Plan, as of the date of the divorce noted above. Benefits will be payable to the Alternate Payee in any form or permissible option otherwise available to the Alternate Payee under the terms of the Plan, including but not limited to a single lump-sum payment.

7. The Alternate Payee will receive the portion of the Plan benefits assigned to the Alternate Payee (the "Alternate Payee's Portion") in a single transfer into an account of his/her designation. If the Plan cannot transfer the Alternate Payee's Portion into an account of his/her designation, then the Plan will open a new account for the Alternate Payee in his/her name and will transfer the Alternate Payee's Portion into this new account.

8. The Alternate Payee will be eligible to receive payment as soon as administratively reasonable following the determination that this order is a Qualified Domestic Relations Order.

9. <u>Death of Participant or Alternate Payee.</u>

    a. If the Participant predeceases the Alternate Payee prior to payment of the Alternate Payee's assigned benefits under the Plan, the Alternate Payee's benefits will not be affected. In the event of the Participant's death, the account balance which remains the property of the Participant will be payable to the Participant's designated beneficiary or in accordance with Plan provisions. This Order does not require the Participant to name the Alternate Payee as the beneficiary for the benefits not assigned to the Alternate Payee.

b. In case of the death of the Alternate Payee prior to distribution of the Alternate Payee's benefits from the Plan, the assigned benefits will be paid to the Alternate Payee's designated beneficiary or, if none, in accordance with Plan provisions.

10. Jurisdiction; Authority to Amend.

a. This matter arises from an action for divorce or legal separation in this Court under the case number set forth at the beginning of this order. Accordingly, this Court has jurisdiction to issue this order.

b. In the event the Plan Administrator determines that this order is not a Qualified Domestic Relations Order, both parties will cooperate with the Plan Administrator in making any changes needed for this order to be accepted by the Plan as a Qualified Domestic Relations Order. This includes signing all necessary documents. For this purpose, this Court expressly reserves jurisdiction over the dissolution proceeding involving the Participant, the Alternate Payee, and the Participant's interest in the Plan.

11. Pursuant to Section 414(p)(3) of the Code and except as provided by Section 414(p)(4), this Order:

a. Does not require the Plan to provide any type or form of benefit, or any option, not otherwise provided under the Plan;

b. Does not require the Plan to provide increased benefits; and

c. Does not require the payment of benefits to an Alternate Payee that is required to be paid to another Alternate Payee under another order previously determined to be a Qualified Domestic Relations Order.

12. For purposes of Sections 402 and 72 of the Code, any Alternate Payee who is the spouse or former spouse of the Participant will be treated as the distributee of any distributions or payments made to the Alternate Payee under the terms of the order and, as such, will be required to pay the appropriate federal, state, and local income taxes on such distributions.

13. <u>Inadvertent Payment</u>.

a. If the Plan inadvertently pays to the Participant any benefit that is assigned to the Alternate Payee pursuant to the terms of this order, the Participant will immediately reimburse the Plan to the extent that the Participant has received such benefit payments and will forthwith pay such amounts so received to the Plan within ten (10) days of receipt.

b. If the Plan inadvertently pays to the Alternate Payee any benefit that is actually payable to the Participant, the Alternate Payee must make immediate reimbursement. The Alternate Payee must reimburse to the extent that he/she has received such benefit payments and will forthwith pay such amount so received to the Plan within ten (10) days of receipt.

14. If the Plan is terminated, the Alternate Payee will be entitled to receive his/her portion of the Participant's benefits as stipulated herein in accordance with the Plan's termination provisions for participants and beneficiaries.

15. All payments made pursuant to this order will be conditioned on the certification by the Alternate Payee and the Participant to the Plan Administrator of such information as the Plan Administrator may reasonably require from such parties to make the necessary calculation of the benefit amounts contained herein.

16. Tax Treatment of Distributions Made Under this Order: For purposes of Section 402(a) and 72(m) of the Internal Revenue Code, any Alternate Payee who is the spouse or former spouse of the Participant will be treated as the distributee of any distribution or payments made to the Alternate Payee under the terms of the Order, and as such, will be required to pay the appropriate federal income taxes on such distribution.

17. The Court finds this Order has been prepared by counsel for the Alternate Payee and reviewed and approved by both the Participant's counsel and by a representative of the Plan prior to its presentation to the Court. **[15]**

    SO ORDERED this _____ day of _____, 20_____.

_____
Judge of _[16]_ Court
_[17]_ County, _[18]_

NOTES ON NEXT PAGE

114

Notes for Qualified Domestic Relations Order ("QDRO"):

[1]   The type of trial court that granted your divorce. This can vary depending on your state but will probably be something like "Superior", "Circuit", or "District".

[2]   The name of the county in which your divorce was granted.

[3]   The name of the state in which your divorce was granted.

[4]   The full name of the plaintiff in the divorce case; either you or your former spouse.

[5]   The full name of the defendant in the divorce case; either you or your former spouse (whichever one of you is not the plaintiff).

[6]   The case number of your divorce case.

[7]   Name of state; same as [3].

[8]   The name of the retirement plan being divided.

[9]   The person whose name is on the account is the "participant".

[10]   The former spouse, who is receiving part of the account, is the "alternate payee".

[11]   The date of the marriage.

[12]   The date the divorce decree was entered.

[13]   The name of the person or entity responsible for administering the retirement plan.

[14]   The amount to be transferred to the alternate payee.

[15]   The last paragraph makes reference to counsel for the respective parties. Be sure to change this language to fit the facts, if one or both of you did not actually have counsel for the process of drafting the QDRO.

[16]   Type of court; same as [1].

[17]   Name of county; same as [2].

[18]   Name of state; same as [3].

Day 13 – Cover Letter to Send QDRO to Judge

_[1]_

Via First Class U.S. Mail:

_[2]_

RE: _[3]_ v. _[4]_.
_[5]_ **Court of** _[6]_ **County**
Case No. _[7]_
Divorce Decree Entered _[8]_

Dear _[9]_,

I am the former spouse of _[10]_. This Court granted our divorce on _[11]_. A copy of this letter is sent to _[12]_.

Paragraph _[13]_ of our divorce decree [14] provides for a portion of my former spouse's retirement account to be transferred to me by qualified domestic relations order ("QDRO"). I have prepared a proposed QDRO, which is enclosed for the Court's consideration.

If it is acceptable, I would appreciate it if you would send me a *certified* copy of the entered QDRO. I have enclosed a self-addressed stamped envelope for this purpose. Upon my receipt of the same, I will forward a regular copy to _[15]_ and send the certified copy to the plan.

Thank you for your attention to this matter. Please contact me at your convenience if you have questions or if I can further assist the Court.

Sincerely,

_[16]_

NOTES ON NEXT PAGE

Notes for Cover Letter to Send QDRO to Judge

[1]   The date of the letter.

[2]   The name and address of the Judge. You would write the Judge's name as (for example) "Hon. John Smith". You should also address the letter specifically to the Judge's secretary, law clerk, or staff attorney, and not directly to the Judge.

[3]   The plaintiff's last name in the divorce case.

[4]   The defendant's last name in the divorce case.

[5]   The type of trial court that granted your divorce ("Superior", "Circuit", etc.).

[6]   The name of the county where your divorce was granted.

[7]   The case number of your divorce.

[8]   The date your divorce decree was "entered" (generally, the date on the clerk's file-stamp on your divorce decree).

[9]   The person to whom you are addressing the letter – probably *not* the Judge directly. See [2].

[10] Your former spouse's name.

[11] The date of your divorce; same as [8].

[12] Your former spouse's name.

[13] You will have to look up the paragraph number from the divorce decree or your settlement agreement that gives you the right to have the QDRO entered.

[14] You may have to change "our divorce decree" to something like "our settlement agreement", as appropriate.

[15] Your former spouse's name.

[16] Your name.

Day 27 – Letter to Former Spouse Requesting Proof of Life Insurance

_[1]_

Via First Class U.S. Mail:

_[2]_

RE: Request for Proof of Life Insurance

Dear _[3]_,

Paragraph _[4]_ of our divorce agreement provides that I have the right to request proof of life insurance from you annually and that you are obligated to provide it to me. Please forward me proof of coverage at your earliest convenience.

Thank you for your attention to this matter. Please contact me at your convenience if you have questions.

Sincerely,

_[5]_

NOTES ON NEXT PAGE

Notes for Letter to Former Spouse Requesting Proof of Life Insurance

[1]   The date of the letter.

[2]   The name and address of your former spouse.

[3]   Your former spouse's first name or nickname.

[4]   Paragraph number from your divorce agreement (be as specific as you can).

[5]   Your name.

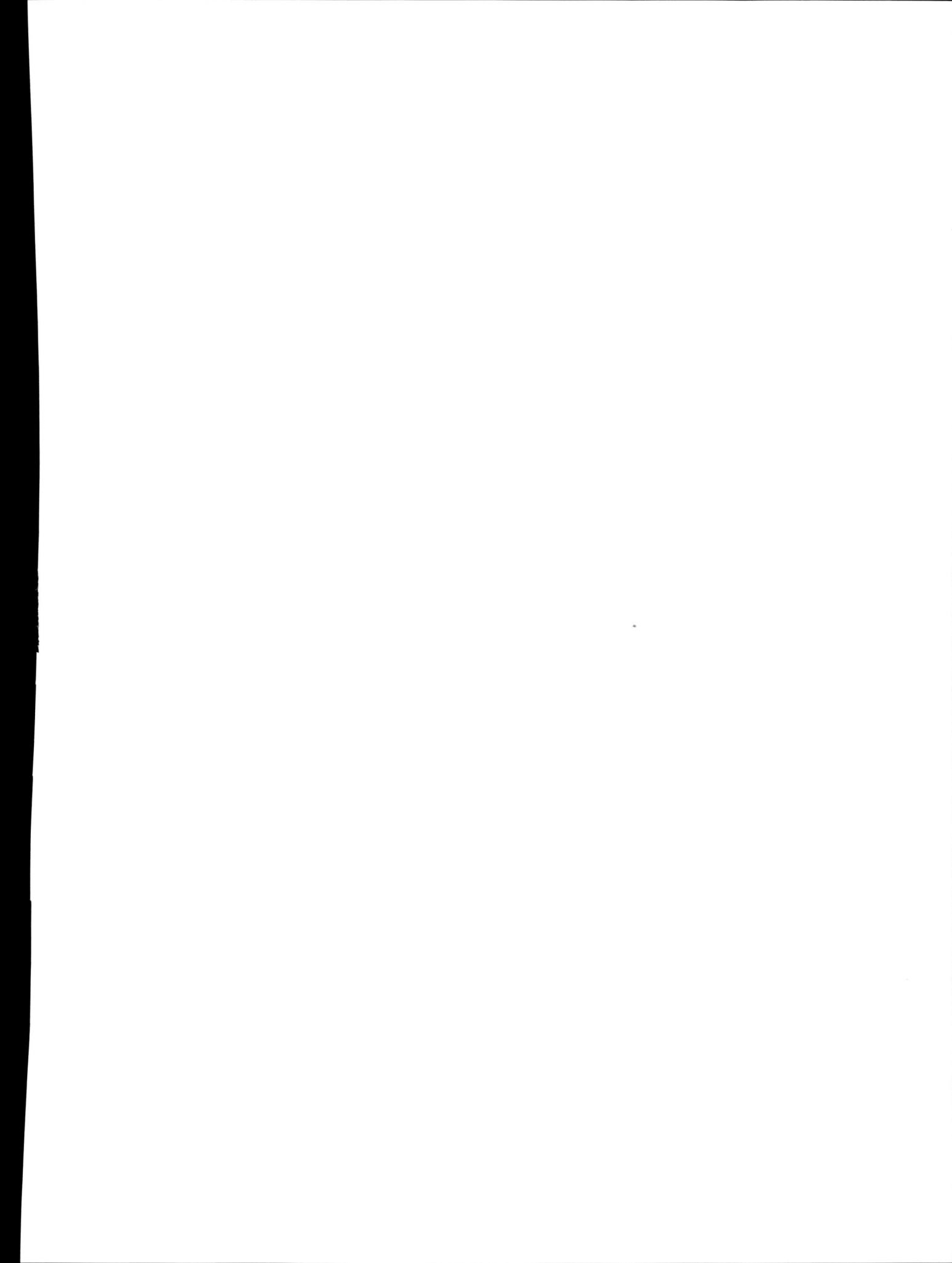

www.ingramcontent.com/pod-product-compliance
Lightning Source LLC
Chambersburg PA
CBHW082104210326
41599CB00033B/6574